# GLOUCESTER GALE

The True Story of the Swordfishing
Schooner *Dorcas*

Dan Fuller

Agile Swordfish Publishing

Cover Design by Brendan Keohane

Line Editing by Ursula DeYoung

This is a work of creative nonfiction

ISBN: 979-8-218-15043-3

Library of Congress Control Number: 2023902233

Agile Swordfish Publishing
Tampa, FL

Dedicated to:

# THEY THAT GO
# DOWN TO THE SEA
# IN SHIPS

# Contents

# Gloucester Gale

# The Imperators

In Portugal, at the beginning of the fourteenth century, Queen Isabella, the princess of Aragon, was deeply moved by the plight of the poor. Against the wishes of her husband, King Denis, she attempted to smuggle bread to those who needed it most in Lisbon. She carefully tried to hide the loaves under her apron, and she almost got away with it, but the king was tipped off by a servant in the bakery who had noticed the bulge. The king accused Isabella of defying his wishes. The queen said a quick prayer to the Holy Ghost. When the king opened her apron, the bread turned miraculously into red roses and a white dove. The roses fell toward the floor, and the white dove flew up into the sky toward heaven. This became known as the Miracle of the Roses.

To give thanks for that miracle from the Holy Ghost, Queen Isabella started an annual tradition in which she would place a silver crown onto the heads of twelve of the common folk in Lisbon, thus elevating them to the rank of Imperator for the day. She would honor her twelve Imperators by hosting them as her guests at an outdoor community supper, where she fed the poor people of Lisbon. Portuguese communities around the world today still practice their own folksy versions of this crowning ceremony and community supper.

# The Portland Gale

Why did the captain leave that night,
Ten thousand voices cry,
Unheedful of such warning;
But there's none left to reply.
He went, he met the blizzard,
No earthly power could save;
And the once fine steamer *Portland*
Now lies quiet 'neath the wave.

*Loss of the Steamer Portland,* Capt. Frederic R. Eldridge

## Saturday, November 26, 1898.

The Gloucester fishing schooner *Mary P. Mesquita,* under the command of Captain Joseph P. Mesquita, was beset by an early blizzard while fishing off the coast of Cape Ann. During that Thanksgiving weekend storm, which would become known as the Portland Gale, the crew of the *Mary P. Mesquita* narrowly avoided being cut in two by the steamer *Portland.* The *Portland* herself was not so fortunate. Nobody knew exactly what happened, but sometime after her near collision with the *Mary P. Mesquita,* the *Portland* foundered with all one hundred and ninety-two of her passengers and crew.

Shortly after the near collision, the heroic captain of the *Mary P. Mesquita,* who was known to everyone in Gloucester as Smokey Joe, led his crew in prayer. The skipper promised that if they made it back home to safety, he would lead them in a solemn procession, dressed in their oilskins, sou'westers, and boots. They would start down at the wharf and from there walk all the way up the hill to the old wooden Portuguese church in their fishing gear. He also promised that they would all bake bread to feed the poor in Gloucester. They kept both of those promises.

* * *

Two years later, in October of 1900, Smokey Joe and the crew of the *Mary P. Mesquita* were fishing on Georges Bank. There they found themselves in a thick fog. It was only right before the impact of the crash that they heard the distress horns. The Cunard cruise liner *Saxonia* smashed right across the bow of the *Mary P. Mesquita*, splitting her in half amidships. Somehow, all of the crew except for one man found their way onto one of the two dories that had been launched immediately before the *Mary P. Mesquita* sank.

Smokey Joe was devastated by the loss of one of his men. He promised, both to his crew and to the Queen of Heaven, that if they all survived the ordeal and made it back to safety, he would commission a silver crown to be made in Portugal, and that he would then donate it to Our Lady of Good Voyage.

His prayer was answered: they were all rescued by the *Saxonia*. The cruise liner had looped around to search for survivors. She found them and gave them safe passage all the way to England. From there Smokey Joe traveled the rest of the way to Lisbon to fulfill his promise, with only two coins in his pocket.

The silver crown he commissioned had eight sides and a silver dove on its crest. Before he brought it back to Gloucester, he took it to Rome and Pope Leo XIII blessed it. Since then, the Crown of the Holy Ghost has been used in at least one crowning ceremony at the church of Our Lady of Good Voyage in Gloucester every year.

# Crown of the Holy Ghost

> The children gather wood,
> And the fathers kindle the fire,
> And the women knead their dough,
> To make cakes to the queen of heaven

*Jeremiah 7:18*

*Tuesday, September 9, 1924.*

The eight surviving Gloucester fishermen from the schooner *Dorcas* walked up the steps into the church of Our Lady of Good Voyage. They wore their oilskins, rubber boots, and yellow sou'wester hats as they walked through the main entryway into the Catholic church. They were there for a reckoning, and for a thanksgiving. They were there to keep a solemn promise they had made while their souls were at peril down to the sea, during the pursuit of swordfish. They had made their promise fourteen days ago to the Queen of Heaven.

The newly rebuilt Portuguese church on Prospect Street was a stone structure with a stucco finish. It had a large hardwood main door in the center. Each of the two front belltowers had a smaller matching door at its base, one to the right and one to the left of the larger central door. Above this main door was a large white scallop shell under a round stained-glass window. On top of each of the two belltowers was a bleached white dome with a golden cross. At the top of the center steeple was a statue, carved by the Italian sculptor Angelo Lualdi, of the Virgin Mary. She held a schooner in her left hand, cradled like the Christ child. This statue was referred to by the locals as the Queen of Heaven. When Gloucester fishermen were in dire need of help, they prayed to her.

The crowning ceremony that day had started at a quarter past eight o'clock in the morning. The eight Gloucester swordfishermen started down at the harbor, dressed in their fishing gear, just like Smokey Joe. They walked up the hill and turned left past the Gorton-Pew Fisheries company, then continued up the hill onto Prospect Street. All along the route were onlookers, lining the streets to watch the curious spectacle. A little further up on the right was Our Lady of Good Voyage. The eight Gloucester fishermen could smell the sweetbread *rosquilhas* baking in the ovens of the Portuguese Club next door. In the church the congregation was already waiting for them, as was Father Francisco G. Martins in the pulpit.

The eight swordfishermen entered the church in pairs, walking two by two through the big front doors. They passed underneath the wooden ship models overhead, adorning the balcony of the choir. They passed by pews filled with the parishioners, and they passed the different Stations of the Cross to the left and right on the outer walls. In between each station was a column, and on each column was the model of a wooden ship, sometimes a schooner, sometimes a beam trawler, seiner, or other type of fishing vessel. One of the model schooners bore the name *Mary P. Mesquita*.

Finally the eight crew-members of the *Dorcas* arrived at the front pews, which had been reserved for them. They knelt, four on the right side in front of the fresco painting of Lisbon Harbor, and four on the left in front of the fresco painting of Gloucester Harbor. In the pew behind them were their family-members; in the next pew were families and friends from the fishing community, such as Captain Fronteiro and Smokey Joe; and behind them were many well-known residents and dignitaries from Gloucester and the other towns of Cape Ann. Captain Howard Blackburn, one of Gloucester's legendary fishermen, sat by himself in the last pew. He held onto his prayer book and hymnal as best he could with the stubs that remained on his hands. Almost all of his fingers had been lost to frostbite during a winter fishing tragedy many years ago.

Father Martins performed the Catholic Mass, and then, after the Eucharist, he carried out the crowning ceremony. The eight thankful survivors knelt before him. In one hand the priest cradled the silver crown commissioned by Smokey Joe, made in Portugal, blessed by the Pope. In the other he held a matching silver staff with a dove on top. He placed the crown onto the head of each man in turn, gently touching the dove on the staff to the dove on top of the crown. For each man, he sang a verse from scripture. "*Veni Creator Spiritus*," he recited aloud, eight times in succession. At the end of the ceremony, the newly crowned Imperators walked out of the church as before, two by two, with their order reversed—last in, first out. They exited the church through the big front doors.

Mary Dahlmer, the daughter of Smokey Joe, sat perched up high in the carillon chamber, lit by the stained-glass window. She played the thirty-one carillon bells, leveraging the sixty-two levers on the clavier and the accompanying foot pedals with the utmost skill, having studied for two years with a pair of Flemish masters. She was playing the first complete set of carillon bells in America, as the first female carillonneur in the country. Balling her fists like a pugilist, she pushed them down forcefully but carefully onto each of the clavier's levers, depending on the note she wanted to play. Each hammer played a different note on a different bell, thanks to the carillon's complex wire machinery. Up in the tower, each bell had a unique pair of names engraved upon it, a Catholic Saint joined with a historically significant Gloucesterman, usually a fisherman who had been lost at sea.

Mary skillfully played the hymn "Scatter Flowers on the Waves" on the carillon, as the eight Imperators and the rest of the congregation walked out of the church into the square.

For the next two hours, the eight Imperators prepared for the community supper. They used the kitchen in the Portuguese Club across the street, making soup with the help of the kitchen staff. They had donated their pay from their swordfishing trip as "God's share" to fund the beef and cabbage for the soup, and they also donated their time to help to prepare the food for the meal.

One hour later, the carillon bells of Our Lady of Good Voyage rang twelve times, signaling noon. The Imperators emerged from the club in pairs, carrying four large pots of soup, two men to a pot. Along the perimeter of the square were four long makeshift dining tables, in between the church and the club. The square was already filled with the residents of Gloucester. Everyone on

Portuguese Hill had brought out their tables and chairs to help set up for the event.

Each pair of Imperators carried their soup pot to a different row of tables. At the center of the square was a smaller table covered with a white cloth and adorned with roses. It supported a wooden platform displaying the Crown of the Holy Ghost, the sacred silver relic that Smokey Joe had brought back from Portugal. Around the platform were stacked one hundred freshly baked *rosquilhas* loaves. They were to be raffled off to the poor later in the day.

Almost all of the people of Gloucester stood in line at one of the square's four stations, with their soup bowls. The eight Gloucester Imperators filled each bowl with a handful of sweet bread and a generous ladle-full of the *Sopas do Espirito Santo*. They continued serving the community for over an hour, until every bowl was filled. In this way, they fulfilled their promise to the Queen of Heaven.

# Down to the Sea

They that go down to the sea in ships,
That do business in great waters;
These see the works of the Lord,
And his wonders in the deep.

*Psalms 107*: 23-24

### *Thursday, August 21, 1924.*

Since the founding of Gloucester three hundred years ago, over eight thousand fishermen have been lost at sea. In 1924, with the year more than halfway over, Gloucester had experienced an unusually uneventful start to the fishing season, with only six fishermen lost so far.

Back in early April, Eldridge Corkum had been lost from the steamer *Fabia S.* Shortly thereafter, three fishermen—Antonio Santos Cortina, Duarte Magellers, and Manuel Natario—were lost when the *Laura Goulart* capsized. George A. Stubert was lost on the *Elsie G. Silva* that same day. And the schooner *Elizabeth W. Nunan* lost Harry Baker, who went overboard from his dory during that same April gale. Since then, the weather had continued to be quite conducive to fishing in Gloucester, Cape Ann, and the New England fisheries.

\* \* \*

Joseph Silveira was born in 1872 on the island of Pico, in the Portuguese archipelago known as the Azores. He came to America when he was twenty-one years old, with all three of his brothers and

13

his mother, Luzia. Tragically, only one of his brothers now remained, his youngest brother, Sebastian, who was also Joseph's first mate. The other two brothers had both been lost to the tragic perils of the maritime trades: first his brother Manuel, in 1913, and then John two years later. Joseph had also lost his father many years before, back in the Azores, in a whaling tragedy, and he was convinced after all of these deaths that the sea was his family's curse.

In Gloucester, as a young man, Joseph had married a dressmaker named Mary Vieira de Freitas. The Silveira family now lived in a Victorian house close to the top of the hill known to the locals as Portuguese Hill. Joseph had established himself early on as one of Gloucester's up-and-coming highliners, with a reputation for highly profitable fishing trips. His family had recently started to enjoy the appurtenances of his commercial fishing success.

Joseph and Mary had four daughters: Maria, Lelia, Genevieve, and Winnifred. Joseph usually didn't wake his daughters when he departed early for a fishing trip, and this morning was no exception. His wife, on the other hand, woke up before he did and had a light breakfast and coffee ready for him before he left. He ate his breakfast, washed up, packed his things, and kissed his wife good-bye. On his way out the door he could hear the familiar sounds as she started to clean up the plates and silverware.

He set out at sunrise. He could see the silver-gray water of Gloucester Harbor down the hill through the trees, and the clock tower of the city hall down the hill to the right. On the left he could see the twin white domes of Our Lady of Good Voyage and the statue on the steeple—the Queen of Heaven. He wore his skipper's hat, a long-sleeved white shirt, denim pants, and suspenders. His rosary beads hung around his neck under his shirt. His duffel bag was slung over his shoulder. He was well above average height for the times, just shy of six feet. He had short, sandy hair that had turned mostly gray, with a matching mustache and hazel eyes, as well as a very dark complexion from spending so much time on the water.

Today he had an eerie feeling. He was known for being a bit superstitious. Like many skippers in the Gloucester fleet, he was adamantly opposed to starting a fishing trip on a Friday; doing so had been thought throughout the ages to invite bad luck onto a crew. On many occasions, his friends and family had overheard him talking about how he "had a feeling" that sometime or other the sea would claim him as a victim. This time, however, he felt different. Prior to today, he had never felt so nervous when leaving home.

He had already decided to call it a season on swordfish and arrange for his schooner to be "changed over." The schooner that he captained, the *Dorcas,* was representative of the small and maneuverable swordfishing boats of that era. Built in 1901 in the Essex shipyard for the Central Wharf Cold Storage Company of Portland, she was 53 feet long from stem to stern and had an 18-foot beam at her widest point, between the port and starboard rails. She could handle an eight-man crew in addition to Joseph. The newest feature of the *Dorcas* was her auxiliary marine engine. Joseph's original plan had been for the *Dorcas* to be changed over this week to go out after cod and haddock. You needed very different types of gear and equipment when you fished for those other commercial species, so it took some time to retrofit the ship. However, his brother and the crew were all dead set against it, so he had agreed to go on one more swordfishing trip.

He opened the fence gate and passed by Burnham's Field to his right. As he walked down the hill, he wondered why the field always flooded during heavy summer rain. Eventually he reached the Melvin H. Perkins apothecary, then turned left onto Prospect Street and walked further down the hill, getting much closer to sea level. He passed Our Lady of Good Voyage on the left and the Portuguese Club on the right. On some of the public buildings, he could see signs for National Defense Day.

Once on Rogers Street, he turned left toward Pew's Wharf in the inner harbor, where he would find the *Dorcas*. He arrived first, followed shortly thereafter by his youngest crew-member, his engineer, Antone "Tone" Rose. Joseph knew Tone's parents; they were family friends who also came from the Azores. He watched intently as the young engineer made his way up the gangway. Tone had short black hair and blue eyes, and was clean-shaven. He was about five feet eight, and he wore a long-sleeved gray shirt, gray overalls, and a matching gray fiddler cap. Although he was lanky and not athletically built, he was surprisingly sure on his feet, and he could claim a good Gloucester fishing pedigree.

Joseph knew he should learn more about the emerging domain of marine motors and engines. However, he had very little interest in all that modern machinery; instead he left it to Sebastian, his younger brother, who was much more enthusiastic about the new technology.

As for Tone, he was new to the occupation of marine engineer; he had lucked his way into the occupation through family connections, but since he was mechanically inclined, it made sense for him to try a new trade: there was a marked shortage of skilled laborers and tradesmen since the end of the Great War. After apprenticing in the fleet, Tone had become qualified to take on engineering jobs as a journeyman, and that was why Joseph had hired him to work on the *Dorcas*.

Earlier this spring, the schooner's auxiliary engine had been installed. Engineering was still a growing field. Only in the past fifteen years had it become profitable to retrofit a fishing schooner with an auxiliary engine. There was an inflection point where the additional cost of the new equipment, fuel, and extra crew-member was offset by the greater catch, resulting in a higher profit. Now most ships in the fleet had at least a retrofitted auxiliary engine, and all the new schooners had one built inboard. In fact, it was essential to have an engine when you were swordfishing, because without one you wouldn't have the maneuverability to hunt for them on the surface.

Joseph joined Tone on the dock, where the young engineer set to the task of loading dozens of barrels of fuel. The skipper helped him. When they finished stowing the last barrel in the engine room, Tone pulled out his big screwdriver. Joseph watched for a few minutes as the young engineer prepared the thirty-horsepower Sterling Fisherman engine. Then he left him to his work and walked up the stairwell to see who else had arrived.

* * *

Sebastian Silveira had already boarded the *Dorcas* when Joseph came topside.

"Mr. Rose is down below in the engine room," Joseph said to his younger brother. "Mr. Nunes and the dory mates should be arriving soon, and so should Doc."

"Got it, brother—er, I mean skipper. I'll make sure they all help Doc with the supplies." As first mate, Sebastian was responsible for guiding the crew while Joseph manned the helm and drove the *Dorcas*.

Sebastian was forty-five years old, five feet eleven, with a medium build. He had brown eyes, curly brown hair with a matching mustache, and darkly tanned skin, just like his brother. He wore a brown paddy cap, a gray sweater, and denim pants. He lived in Cambridge with his wife, Bella, and his two young daughters, Olga and Alice. The youngest of the four Silveira brothers, he had been just a boy of fourteen when his family came from the Azores to the United States.

At first the brothers had fished commercially out of Boston and then Gloucester, for cod, haddock, pollock, and sometimes mackerel. As the oldest brother, Joseph had soon made a name for himself, eventually becoming a captain and settling in as one of the most respected skippers in the Gloucester fishing fleet. Sebastian was not quite as seasoned as his brother. He was still deciding whether he wanted fishing to be his career or not. For now, it was a profitable trade and supported his family.

Last summer, the two brothers had decided to try their hands at swordfishing, applying the same methods used in whaling in the Azores but on a different scale. Sebastian was very eager for this particular trip; he truly enjoyed swordfishing. Not only was it profitable, but the weather was milder now than at any other time of the year, and there was something exhilarating about the experience of catching just one giant fish at a time; you never felt the same when catching a schooner full of cod or mackerel.

His older brother had wanted to make the safe bet and call it quits on swordfish, but Sebastian and the other crew-members had voted against that because it had been such a successful swordfishing season. They had all convinced their skipper to make one more try at swordfish, in the hopes of one more profitable trip.

Sebastian was topside when the striker arrived. Domingoes Nunes was the tallest member of the crew, at six feet two inches tall. He had broad shoulders and long arms, with a wide wingspan. He had very dark skin, even darker than Sebastian and his brother, and dark brown eyes. His brown hair was short, and he was clean-shaven. He wore black pants and a brimmed hat, as well as a long-sleeved blue shirt with a patch on the left elbow; the right sleeve had been cut off above the elbow, exposing his large muscular forearm. This tall swordfishermen from Cape Verde was one of the most experienced men in all of the swordfishing fleet. His prowess in the Gloucester fleet had already become legendary. He had learned the art of swordfishing a number of years ago, after a long career as a whaler in the New Bedford whaling fleet. Now, like many of the other successful Portuguese fishermen, he lived on Portuguese Hill with his wife, Rosella. Sebastian thought they made an interesting couple. Rosella was as tall as her husband, beautiful, and quite voluptuous. Truth be told, Sebastian thought Rosella was the most beautiful woman in all of Gloucester—but that was a secret he kept to himself.

As the striker on the *Dorcas*, it was Domingoes—and only Domingoes—who harpooned the swordfish. This was a dangerous job, and Sebastian and Joseph needed someone reliable to perform it; that was why Sebastian had convinced his brother that they needed to hire Domingoes, who had established himself as one of the best strikers in the fleet. He rarely missed, and he was worth every penny of his "lay"—his share of the profits.

Sebastian helped the striker carry aboard his ash-wood harpoons, which Domingoes called *arpãos* in his native Portuguese. Domingoes had the most pronounced Portuguese accent of the crew-members. The striker spoke English well, but he had a tendency to revert to Portuguese out of habit. After stowing his gear in his locker in the forecastle, Domingoes unloaded his whalecraft, a leather satchel full of harpoon tips and other tools of the trade.

He pulled a horseshoe out of the leather bag and said to Sebastian, "I have two loves. Number one is my beloved Rosella, and number two is my good-luck charm." Sebastian knew what was coming next. They walked through the door of the forecastle, and Sebastian climbed up the rigging on the mainmast to the crosstree, one of his favorite vantage points. From that spot he watched his striker stretch his arms out over the bowsprit of the *Dorcas* and lash the horseshoe to its base with a length of manilla rope, to serve as their good-luck talisman on the trip.

\* \* \*

The first of the dory mates to arrive was Joseph Silva—known by his surname to everyone on the *Dorcas* to distinguish him from the skipper, and all the other crew members who were also named Joseph. He was shorter than the Silveira brothers and had black hair and brown eyes. He wore a white striped shirt with gray wool pants. He lived close by in a small fisherman's rental house, and had recently married a beautiful young woman named Julia. He was the nephew of the skipper and the first mate, but they didn't give him any special treatment when it came to his pay. The three older and more experienced dory mates were each entitled to a full lay. Silva, being newer to the trade, was entitled to earn only a three-quarter lay, the traditional share for a journeyman in the fishing union. Although he had some experience in other forms of fishing, this was Silva's first time going down to the sea for swordfish.

As the crew-members arrived, the first thing they did was find their lockers by the bunks in the forecastle. Each man had his own locker for his gear and personal effects. Inside each one was a hook to store their foul-weather fishing gear—oilskins, sou'westers, and boots. In addition to the lockers, there was a common slop chest containing many spare pairs of rubber boots and extra cold-weather gear, such as wool hats and mittens.

Soon Silva was joined by Joseph Merico, an older, Sicilian-born fisherman who was quick to find the humor in any situation but also quick to anger. He was the oldest dory mate, at age thirty-nine. He had a round face and broad shoulders, and he immediately started to share his wisdom with Silva as they stowed their gear. "Thursday is a good day to head down to the sea," he said. "Never leave on a Wednesday or a Friday—especially not on Friday! Everyone knows that's bad luck." Merico claimed the first locker and stowed his cribbage board in it with the rest of his personal effects. "Stick with me, kid. I'm one of the best swordfish killers in the fleet," he bragged.

Joseph Brown and John Murray arrived next. They were almost exactly the same size, but while Brown had a beard, Murray had a waxed handlebar mustache.

The four dory mates met in the forecastle, by the four bunks and eight lockers. The bunks were all the way forward, with two on each side. By design, the crew could sleep in shifts of four at a time, while the rest of the crew would be topside on watch. Each bunk had a shelf over the headboard and a straw mattress covered with a fitted sheet, a wool blanket, and a pillow. There were two additional bunks in the captain's cabin, reserved for the skipper and the first mate. The rest of the crew, including the striker, the cook, and the engineer, would share the bunks in the forecastle.

"Did you see any women on your way down to the boat, lad?" Murray asked Silva.

"Not a one. There wasn't anyone on the streets when I got

here," Silva answered.

"That's good. It's a bad omen to have any sort of encounter with a lady on the way down to a fishing boat."

"And tell us, Murray, when was the last time you had an encounter with a lady?" Merico teased. It was common for the men to engage in crass humor, though not when they were in earshot of the skipper.

* * *

The cook was the next man to arrive—an affable man named Joseph Souza, known as Doc. He had big ears, brown eyes, brown curly hair, and a bushy mustache. He wore a white apron over a white shirt, with a matching white hat.

Sebastian was good friends with the cook, who had been working in the Gloucester fleet for many years. His daily wage was good, as determined by the union. In the event of one of the crew getting seriously hurt and needing medical assistance, he had also been trained in first aid and knew some basic emergency procedures, such as stitching up a deep wound—hence his nickname. It was common for men to have double duties on a commercial fishing vessel.

"Greetings, Doc," Sebastian said. "We need to get moving and bring aboard all the supplies."

Waiting for them on the dock were many sacks of dried goods, along with barrels and crates full of foodstuffs, all with the logo of the Atlantic Supply Company. Captain Jerry Fronteiro, the owner of the *Dorcas,* had arranged for the delivery of the supplies for the trip, and he joined them on the wharf shortly after Doc arrived. He wore a dark suit and bowler hat, and took care of all the business arrangements while the crew got the *Dorcas* ready.

Sebastian double-checked the supplies against the order until he was satisfied that everything had been delivered. Keeping a crew of nine Gloucestermen well-fed on a fourteen-day trip took hundreds of dollars' worth of food and potables, as well as other crucial supplies like fuel for the lanterns and the ship's stove. The most strenuous task was loading the dozens of barrels of potable water. After that, Sebastian and Doc each carried aboard two large glass bottles containing lemon essence, an essential component of a fisherman's diet. There was also some fresh fruit, plenty of dried and canned fruit, and jars of jellies and jam.

Next they attended to the rest of the dried goods and other bulk items, such as barrels of "hard tack"—dried seafaring biscuits; sacks of starchy foods such as oats, potatoes, and rice; and crates of essential pantry items. For breakfast there were sacks of oatmeal, loaves of bread, and something special for Sunday—the secret ingredients needed to make the Portuguese donuts known as *filhós*. The cook pulled out a small flask of whiskey from his pocket. "What a fiasco it will be if the skipper finds out about my secret donut ingredient," he said.

Sebastian laughed. Most of the skippers in the fleet, including Joseph, had a strict no-alcohol policy, even when Prohibition was not in place. Sebastian, however, was more inclined to look the other way when alcohol was used for cooking purposes.

Now it was time to load the massive amounts of protein needed for a crew of nine hard-working and hungry fishermen: dried beef, smoked pork and ham, and plenty of salted cod, or *bacalhau* in Portuguese. "My favorite ingredient," Doc said. "I know 365 different ways to cook *bacalhau*, one for each day of the year."

"That's good, because I could easily eat *bacalhau* for a year straight," Sebastian said.

Next they loaded all the eggs, bacon, and *linguiça*, a spicy smoked and cured sausage, and after that many crates of canned goods. At last Sebastian grabbed the final crate, which was full of chewing tobacco, dried tobacco, rolling papers, matches, playing cards, a spare cribbage board, bars of soap, bars of chocolate, and the latest issues of the new magazine *Weird Tales,* which in recent months had become a popular distraction among the Gloucester fishermen.

Doc's last task was to carry on board a stew pot full of something he had cooked in advance. Sebastian could smell the comforting aroma of a familiar Portuguese stew and hoped it was going to be their dinner tonight.

"Looks like everything is bung up and bilge free," Doc said.

With all the gear, fuel, food, water, and other essentials stowed, Sebastian instructed him to keep an eye open for the ice delivery, so the cook remained on the lookout topside.

\* \* \*

One hour before their departure, the Cape Pond Ice Company made their delivery, a few minutes earlier than planned.

Doc and Sebastian corralled the whole crew to help load the ice onto the *Dorcas*.

"Don't you drop any of them ice blocks, you lumpers," Doc admonished the men.

The crew worked together to load the heavy blocks into the ice room. It took every one of them to get it done. After they finished, the cook brought down all the perishables that needed to be kept cold. On the last trip down, he had a watermelon tucked under one arm.

Now Joseph, standing at the helm astern, gave the command to head out to sea. He ordered all hands on deck, except for Tone, who stayed down below in the engine room. When Tone had started the engine and Sebastian had instructed the crew to pull in all the lines and push off, Joseph steered the *Dorcas* out of the harbor. Soon the schooner moved into the channel, under power from the newly installed marine engine.

The crew was in great spirits; they could feel the strong breeze blowing west from the mainland. "Wind from the west, fishing is best!" Joseph called to them.

After a little while, when they had exited the harbor and passed the shoal, Joseph told Sebastian to go below and let Tone know that it was time to go to full power. They would head into the North Atlantic with a course toward Nantucket, past Provincetown on the tip of Cape Cod.

With Gloucester Harbor disappearing in the distance, Joseph gave the command for his sail plan. It was time to take advantage of the favorable westerly winds. "Full sail," he shouted.

Sebastian supervised the men as they shut down the motor and raised the main sail, followed by the foresail and the riding sail, and lastly all three jibs, including the jumbo.

Now under full sail, with the wind blowing steadily from the west, the *Dorcas* moved at full speed toward Provincetown. From there they would turn left toward Georges Bank. The 150-mile trip would take them about twenty hours, given the prevailing winds.

This was when Joseph felt the most at ease; he was always a bit uncomfortable when they were under engine power. He had spent his entire career mastering the traditional maritime and navigational arts, and he was used to being the expert. He did not like having to be dependent on the engineer.

* * *

Mary Silveira was born in Gloucester in 1877. She was now forty-six years old. Her parents had both come from the Azorean island of Faial, the next island over from Pico. More than half of the residents of Gloucester at that point had family ties to the Azores.

She had met Joseph in Gloucester when she was still a young woman, working as a dressmaker while Joseph was still making a name for himself as a fisherman. They got married and tried right away to start a family, but at first they were beset by sorrow. They lost their first child, Joseph, in infancy in 1897. Their second child, Beatrice, died before her second birthday. Sadly, that was not an uncommon tragedy at the time. Fortunately, their next four children, all daughters, were blessed with good health. Mary often wondered if it had bothered Joseph not to have a son. They never spoke about it.

After their oldest surviving daughter was born, Mary always referred to Joseph as "Pa," and all of their children referred to her as "Mama." Maria, called Birdie, was the oldest daughter. She was about to turn twenty-one, later that autumn. Mary knew how hard it would be for her to see Birdie leave home at the end of the summer, though she had already gotten used to Birdie being away in college, studying music in Boston. She was happy that Birdie had received a good education, and she was especially proud that her daughter had earned a scholarship. Birdie was looking forward to a promising career in music. Mary herself had never considered her job in the dressmaking factory as a career, and she had stopped working after she got married. Since then she had been a full-time homemaker.

Lelia was the second oldest daughter. Everyone called her Le. She was free-spirited and independent; nobody ever told Le what to do, and she and Birdie were always arguing.

Genevieve came next; she had turned thirteen earlier that month. Her distinguishing feature was her bright red hair, and her nickname was Kiddo. She was very outgoing and got involved in lots of activities, such as the Girl Scouts. Mary did her best to encourage Kiddo in all her interests.

Their youngest daughter was Winnifred, known as Winnie. She was five, going on six, and quite precocious. Because she was so much younger than the other three girls, Mary paid special attention to her, often playing games with her youngest daughter.

On Thursday morning, Mary was in her kitchen preparing breakfast. She put a pot of water on the stove and lit it. While the water gradually came to a boil, she fried some bacon in a pan and toasted some *bolos*, a type of Portuguese muffin similar to an English muffin but much sweeter. When breakfast was ready, she called to her daughters: "Breakfast is ready, girls! Come now, Birdie, Le, Kiddo, Winnie. Come and eat before it gets cold."

Within a minute, all four of her daughters had converged upon the kitchen to fuel up with the morning meal on that late-summer day.

* * *

Now that the *Dorcas* was under full sail on her way to Georges Bank, Sebastian had work to do. He supervised the crew as they inspected the schooner's gear, making sure everything was ready for tomorrow, when they would arrive at the fishing grounds. Then he asked Merico to take Silva under his wing as he inspected the dories.

Merico agreed, and Sebastian could hear the older dory mate providing earnest instruction to his nephew: "Each dory should have two pairs of oars. These are really good oars. You can tell because they're made of ash wood. And this is the rest of the gear for each dory. Two pairs of thole pins. You need a backup pair because nervous novices like you have a bad habit of dropping these babies overboard. Ha! Dory compass, in case we get separated from the *Dorcas*. Gaff, pretty much self-explanatory. Knife. And, last but not least, the one piece of equipment we hope we never need to use: the scoop you'll use for bailing. Ha!"

They turned their attention to the dozen barrels and tubs on the deck, six on the outer sides of each of the two dory nests, spread out along the rails.

"See how the rope is coiled in the tubs? That's so it will come out clean when the barrel is thrown overboard, not catching onto anything, or anyone! Your job is to splash water on the rope as it spins out, so it doesn't start to burn. And when you're throwing barrels, make sure that you always keep your legs clear of the ropes. That would be a terrible way to go overboard. Ha!"

Each of the tubs and barrels was labeled *Dorcas* in red lettering and numbered from one to twelve. "I like to make sure we have a hundred feet of rope coiled inside each tub," Merico told Silva, "because you need a bit of time—you don't want to throw the barrel overboard immediately. You need to allow enough time to make sure the barb has set deeply in the fish. And you also need to check twice to make sure the rope is clear of the striker's leg, as well as your own. A great striker is a rare breed, and the last thing the skipper would want is for us to get careless and have Domingoes go overboard with one of the kegs."

"Is that why we always sheath a knife on our shoulder straps?" Silva asked.

"Yes, but let's hope none of us ever has to cut ourselves free of a rope that's fouled up around our feet after it's pulled us overboard. Now, you'll need to have the rope in every tub, all twelve of them, coiled up and ready to go every morning. After each run, recoil them to get them ready for the next run. Sometimes we catch more than two swordfish, but since we only have two pairs of dory mates, we can only launch two dories at a time. The dories always have to go back out to find the cast-off barrels—but only after they bring the first two swordfish back. The other two dories are backups, in case there's a problem with one. You'd be surprised how often we lose them; sometimes the swordfish can do a lot of damage."

"Couldn't we go out with more than four dory mates?" Silva asked.

"On a larger schooner, like one of those really big knockabouts, they might have up to eight dories and sixteen dory mates. But those big schooners aren't maneuverable enough for swordfishing, and knockabouts don't have a bowsprit, so it's much harder to harpoon something. They're better suited for dory trawling, and they're great for shacking. The *Dorcas,* on the other hand, is quite maneuverable, but she's only big enough for an eight-to nine-man crew. If we added more men, we wouldn't have enough room for the swordfish. And if we used a bigger schooner, we wouldn't be agile enough to harpoon as many. So little sworders like the *Dorcas* are ideal."

Merico pointed out the pairs of dories on the port and starboard sides, stacked neatly into each other and tied down with two ropes and four cleats. "We keep each pair nested on the topside, and we paint them with the same red and white color scheme, a fresh coat every season. The barrels too, although the barrels don't last as long as the dories do. After each trip I inspect them for leaks and touch up the paint. Sometimes we have to plug leaks at sea, with pitch."

As Merico mentored the greenhorn, the *Dorcas* kept sailing southeast, toward the tip of Cape Cod.

Later that evening, they took a break for dinner. Doc carried the stew pot full of *cozido*, which he had warmed up on the stove, to the forecastle to serve the crew. On most ships in the Gloucester fleet, the captain and the first mate would take their meals separately. Some of the older and more traditional skippers maintained a strict policy of not fraternizing with the crew, but Joseph and Sebastian believed that was an archaic way of thinking; they knew that the camaraderie and communal feeling created by taking meals together would pay big dividends. And though, on larger ships in the fleet, the meals were served in shifts, since the *Dorcas* had a smaller crew they all ate together whenever they could.

Doc deftly served each man a helping of the traditional Azorean slow-cooked stew, which consisted of braised beef, pork, chicken, and *linguiça*, along with cabbage, kale, carrots, potatoes, and yams. Even the non-Portuguese crew-members left the table satiated that evening.

\* \* \*

Birdie Silveira had just finished dinner with her family. Only her Pa was missing. He was down to the sea swordfishing and would not be back for two more weeks. Now Birdie was getting ready to go out for the evening. At twenty years old she was still diminutive in stature but quite beautiful and graceful. She was passionate about music and had become a talented musician and singer after studying music at the New England Conservatory in Boston. In Gloucester the locals referred to her fondly as the Portuguese Nightingale. But that wasn't how she had gotten the nickname "Birdie." As a toddler, when she was first starting to talk, her parents had often heard her making high-pitched chirping noises, like a little bird.

Birdie had decided to spend this Thursday night with some of her friends at the Elks Hall, at a concert and dance. She put up her curled hair, donned her pearl necklace, and pinned on a fancy fan hat. Then she said good-bye to her Mama and walked out the front door.

As she crossed Gloucester to get to the Hall, she thought how much fun it was going to be to listen to live music and go dancing with her friends. She was an outgoing girl and always enjoyed social events.

When she arrived, she saw her friend Mary Dahlmer with her husband. Mary was also an avid fan of all things musical, though not nearly as outgoing as Birdie.

"How are you, Birdie?" Mary inquired.

"Oh, I'm doing fine. I'm glad to get out of the house, away from my pesky sisters."

So, while her father was heading out to sea with the crew of the *Dorcas*, Birdie lost herself in the evening's musical performances. First four of her friends performed a series of songs for piano and violin. Then the well-known local musician George Steele captivated the crowd with some solo performances. Afterward a light meal was served, and then the young adults of Gloucester leaped up to dance.

Birdie convinced Mary to join her out on the dance floor. Birdie partnered with one of the eligible young gentlemen who had come alone to the dance, while Mary danced with her husband.

"I feel so awkward—I'm not much of a dancer," Mary said.

"Neither is anyone else here! You'll be fine," Birdie assured her.

Mary followed her husband's lead, while Birdie and her partner did the foxtrot.

"Which song is this one, Mary?"

"'Carolina Mammy,' of course," Mary said.

A few minutes later, Birdie and her partner passed by in the other direction, and Birdie asked Mary about the new song.

"This one is 'Bambalina,'" Mary said. She was gradually becoming more comfortable as she danced with her patient husband.

The band played "Wildflower," "Who's Sorry Now?" and "Yes! We Have no Bananas." They finished the set with a swinging rendition of "Sunkist Rose."

By the time Birdie returned home, everyone else in the house was already fast asleep.

* * *

The *Dorcas* sailed through the night. The crew slept in shifts. Joseph decided to take the first turn at the helm, while his younger brother slept in one of the bunks in the captain's cabin. The other seven men also took turns, with three men topside at all times to help the helmsman while the other four slept in the bunks in the forecastle.

At eleven o'clock, Joseph was relieved topside by his younger brother. Once down in the captain's cabin, the first thing he did was update his log book by the light of the lantern. He made note of the date they had sailed, the names of all his crew-members, and their intended course. Then he shut off the lantern and tried to get a bit of sleep.

The *Dorcas* rocked back and forth in a calm cadence as she continued her way toward Georges Bank. Joseph had a vivid dream. He found himself adrift in a dory, alone and with no oars. What was he to do? The viscous sea was covered in a dark ooze—a significant fish kill, all around him. The thick *ichthyo* smell of death permeated the muck and the slime. Then, in the distance ahead of him, there was a brief but violent disturbance in the water. A giant orange tentacle emerged from below the surface with a gurgle. The long monstrous appendage crashed down onto his dory.

Joseph awoke at the moment of impact. There would be no more sleep for him tonight.

# Georges Bank

Two hundred miles to the south-southeast
On George's the billows foam like yeast.
O'er shallow banks, where on every side
Lies peril of billow, shoal, and tide.
There, riding like sea-gulls with wings at rest,
Cape Ann's swift schooners the sharp seas breast,
With their straining cables reaching down
Where the anchors clutch at the sea-sands brown.

*On George's Bank,* C.W. Hall

### *Friday, August 22, 1924.*

J oseph did not sleep well after the dream, and so he arose early, not as refreshed as he could have been. In his groggy state he looked out at the sea ahead, from his position at the helm. The sun had not yet fully risen, but slowly the morning emerged and replaced the night. He checked their position using the charts and the sextant. He wanted to give some instructions to his brother and the rest of the crew to ensure that everything would be ready for their first day of swordfishing, but his brother was nowhere to be found. *Why is it that, when all the charts came out, Sebastian is always somewhere else? Joseph thought.*

The *Dorcas* was on pace to arrive at the Great South Channel of Georges Bank ahead of schedule, shortly after breakfast. The sky was a clear blue, with not a cloud to be seen. Joseph knew Georges Bank well; he fished there often. It was a plateau that contained 8,500 square miles of shoals, ridges, and countless canyons, some thought to be as deep as fifty fathoms. This natural environment supported a thriving ecosystem of marine life, and at this time of year the swordfish were passing through, feeding upon the abundance both near the surface in the shoals and down deep in the trenches.

A pleasant breakfast scent rose up onto the deck. Curious to find out what the cook was up to, Joseph went down to the galley. He watched as Doc added some fuel to the Mascot cook stove, its brand name forged onto the firebox door; matching pilot wheels were forged onto each side.

"Do you need any help with anything?" Joseph asked as he poured himself some coffee.

"I've got everything under control, don't you worry, skipper," Doc replied.

In one pan he fried the bacon, in the other he scrambled some eggs. Then he toasted some bread directly on the stove top and brewed more coffee in the kettle.

When the food was cooked, Joseph helped him carry the pans over to the forecastle. On their next trip they brought the toast, with butter and jam, and the coffee.

After saying grace, the crew fueled up for a long, busy day of swordfishing. While they ate their breakfast, Joseph complimented the sailing skills of the crew and his first mate. "That was some of the best sailing I've seen in a while, men. We made it down here in near record time. Worthy of a crew racing for the Esperanto Cup."

"Do you think they'll have another International Fishermen's Cup race this year?" Brown asked.

"I hope so," Murray said. "We've had their number lately. Those damned bluenoses up in Nova Scotia can only beat Gloucester when they're cheating."

"Bluenose, that's funny!" Merico laughed. "It's 'cause the weather is so cold up there."

"It's supposed to be a race for real sailors, not real cheaters," Sebastian added.

"Well, in some ways the no-holds-barred spirit is what sets it apart from hoity-toity races like the Lipton Cup," Merico said.

"I don't really follow the fishermen's races. What happened last year?" Silva asked.

"The schooner *Columbia* should have won it last October," Sebastian told him. "The schooner *Bluenose* committed a foul in the second race. Captain Walters sailed the *Bluenose* home in protest of the foul call, but Captain Ben Pine of the *Columbia* declined the cup. They wanted to win it out there on the water. Even though that wasn't a great race, it was great sportsmanship on Captain Pine's part."

"I'll tell you what was a great fishermen's race," Murray said. "Four years ago in 1920, when Gloucester's *Esperanto* beat the *Delawana*. She won the first two races by big margins. It wasn't even close. Captain Welsh beat Himmelman both times easily. The *Esperanto*, now she was a fast schooner. Fastest in the world, I'd wager."

"I bet the *Columbia* could beat her," Merico said. "I hope she races again this fall."

When Joseph and the crew had finished their breakfast, Doc cleared the table and the men got ready for their day.

"Back to work, men," the skipper told his crew. "I want to reach Georges Bank early enough to get in at least one good run before lunch." For the next thirty minutes, the dory mates performed double duty, being sailors as well as fishermen. They unfurled sails, hoisted sails, doused sails, swung and lowered booms, tied knots. Their every action was based on a command from their skipper, often relayed through Sebastian. Usually two men were up at the foremast and another two were at the main mast.

Then they switched into dory-mate mode, doing the heavy lifting to get ready for swordfishing and rowing out after the swordfish in the dories. They moved equipment from one place to another as needed, inspected fishing gear, and scrubbed the decks and tables. In all their tasks they moved around like clockwork—a well-oiled maritime machine under the command of one of the most seasoned and stalwart skippers in the Gloucester fleet.

The dory mates always seemed to be on the move. Merico was the most experienced in the bunch. He had been swordfishing as a young man back in Sicily and was the *de facto* leader of the crew. Today he worked topside, paired up with Silva at the foremast.

"Always remember," he told Silva, "we live by the dory mate's code out here. We're all in this together."

"You mentioned that earlier," Silva said. "What exactly is the code?"

"It means we always look out for each other, and we have

each other's backs. This is a dangerous job. Don't be afraid to ask for help. What we have, we have to share."

"Got it," Silva said. "And thanks for all the advice."

"Sure, no problem, greenhorn. That's also part of the code. But watch out for those two over there," Merico added quietly as he pointed at the other two dory mates. "I don't trust those two devils as far as I can throw them."

Brown and Murray were topside by the main mast. Both of them were seasoned dory mates with lots of fishing and sailing experience.

"Have you ever worked for a Portuguese skipper before?" Brown asked the other man.

"Not before this summer," Murray answered. "The *Dorcas* is my first. Although technically this schooner is owned by a Sicilian— it's just the skipper who is Portuguese."

"It's my first time too. I'm not sure how I feel about it."

"Well, they seem to know what they're doing, and I'm making good money. We haven't had a broken trip with them yet."

"That's true. So far so good, but sometimes all it takes is one unexpected storm."

\* \* \*

Birdie had her morning tea after breakfast while she read the local newspaper. She was saddened to learn of the death of Francis Loud, the well-known band-leader of the Gloucester Cornet Band. She thought back to the many times she had enjoyed performances led by that venerable 91-year-old conductor. Music was her passion, and she knew virtually every local band.

She livened up at learning the happy news of Margaret Anderson, one of the oldest residents on Cape Ann, who had yesterday celebrated her ninety-fifth birthday with friends and family. She didn't know Mrs. Anderson, but she found the story to be uplifting nonetheless.

Birdie folded up the paper after she finished her tea. Le reached for it, but Birdie blocked her by putting her hand down on the paper.

"I'm not done reading that yet," she lied.

"Fine, I'll just sit here and drink my coffee while I wait for you to finish," Le said.

"I don't know how you can drink coffee. A lady should prefer tea."

"I like to do what Pa does: drink coffee in the morning, tea in the afternoon."

"So I suppose you're going to take up swordfishing too, just like Pa?" Birdie quipped.

"I just might," Le snapped. "And let me tell you, I can't wait for you to go away to school. How many more days until you leave?"

"Believe you me, that day can't come soon enough."

"Good luck finding a man up at that fancy music college."

"I'm going there for a lot more than just finding a man. But I suppose the importance of a good education is lost on you. Good luck with your future in swordfishing. I hope you have a long and prosperous career."

The two sisters bickered for the better part of the morning.

* * *

After breakfast, Joseph went to speak with his young engineer. He reviewed the finer points of swordfishing, emphasizing that Tone needed to have the engine working at peak performance during both the mid-morning and the late-afternoon swordfish runs, as the broadbills basked on the surface during their migration.

"I need to know I can count on you, Mr. Rose," Joseph said anxiously.

"I'll have her ready for each run," Tone assured him. "You can count on me."

Next it was time to talk to the striker, Domingoes. Joseph had a brief conference topside with him and Sebastian. They confirmed their basic signals and locations: Sebastian would be up in the crosstree on the main mast as the spotter, while Domingoes would be the striker out in front on the "pulpit" and the end of the bowsprit, and the skipper would be at the helm, steering based on Sebastian's signals.

After their meeting, Sebastian headed below and Joseph said, "I need to talk to you about something, Mr. Nunes."

"Yes, what is it, skipper?"

"We've been having a good summer, and you've proven yourself to be one of the best strikers in the fleet. Going forward, we'll be increasing your share to one and a quarter."

"Thank you, skipper!" Domingoes exclaimed. "My Rosella will be thrilled. Thank you."

"Well-deserved, Mr. Nunes," Joseph said as they shook hands.

Having a share of one and a quarter was reserved for the most experienced and loyal crew-members. On this trip, the only other crew-member with that share was Sebastian. All the rest of the crew would be given one full share, except for Silva with his three-quarter journeyman's share. The cook and engineer didn't get shares; instead they were paid a daily rate. After the trip, it was customary for all of the men to donate a portion of their pay as "God's share" to their churches.

On a typical two-week swordfishing trip, the *Dorcas* averaged forty swordfish, which, when dressed, would bring about 12,500 pounds of swordfish to the market. The current market price was seventeen cents a pound. When you factored in approximately $525 for food, gear, and fuel, as well as the daily wages of the cook and the engineer, the *Dorcas* netted an average profit of $1,600 per trip. Captain Fronteiro, as owner, would claim half of that profit, the skipper would earn a quarter share, and the remainder would be divided among the crew according to their shares. By Joseph's calculation, the additional quarter share for Domingoes could increase the striker's average wage per trip from $80 to $100, and on a really good trip the raise would be even more substantial.

As the *Dorcas* approached the Great South Channel, Joseph examined the charts and used the sextant to calculate angles. He checked the compass and plotted the course. Sebastian took one look at the navigational equipment and walked away in the opposite direction. Joseph said nothing, though he noticed that his brother had reversed course. He gave the order to start the engine and douse the sails, then watched as his brother supervised the crew.

The wind had picked up a bit, and there was a light chop. As he manned the wheel, Joseph reflected on his long fishing career, which had started many years ago in his homeland of the Azores. Now he was one of the most respected captains in Gloucester and a Master Mariner in the fleet, as well as a member of the Holy Name Society, the Portuguese fraternity of the United States. He had first become a skipper for the Boston market in 1904, at a relatively young age. His first schooner was named after Birdie, who had been born the year prior. A few years later, in 1909, he took command of a larger schooner, the *Mary DeCosta*, and started his longstanding business relationship with Captain Fronteiro, who was the owner of both the *Mary DeCosta* and the *Dorcas*.

Young Silva, with some time on his hands, approached Joseph and Sebastian at the helm. "What was it like growing up in the Azores?" he asked.

"Well, I was born there and grew up there, but I became a man here in Gloucester," Sebastian replied. "I could never go back to live there, even though I remember Pico with fondness. We left the Azores for a reason, for a better life. There is one word that says it all: *saudade*. It's hard to translate. It's like *fado* music, but without all the singing. It's that feeling of sadness we all get when we lose something valuable and know we can never get it back."

"How is it better in Gloucester?" Silva asked.

"Well, for starters, there's a lot more economic opportunity here. In the Azores there were only a few privileged noblemen, and then the rest of us. There were no opportunities for women at all, whereas here in America women can vote in elections and even go to college. Also, in the Azores all the important decisions were made by politicians in Lisbon. We never had self-determination."

"God-damned Lizzies!" Doc broke in, walking toward them from the galley. "Always telling us what to do."

"Watch the blasphemy," Joseph commanded sternly. "Although I agree with you."

"Lizzies?" Silva inquired.

"That's what we called the powers that be in Lisbon. We were really no more than a colony to be exploited." Sebastian spoke grimly, but then he changed his tone, becoming more lighthearted. "And don't get me going on all the natural disasters! There were the volcanic eruptions and all those earthquakes." He shook a nearby barrel with his hand, and Silva laughed.

"I guess that since all our family is now here in America, there's no one left to go back and visit," Silva said.

"That's true—I can't think of anyone who's still there except for some distant cousins; and I'm not even certain I can remember their names," Sebastian said.

Joseph felt it was time to focus on the matter at hand. "This is our first summer on the *Dorcas*," he explained to his nephew. As he spoke, he put on his skipper's hat. Even with his dark complexion, on summer days like this he preferred to wear his hat when the sun rose overhead. "Swordfishing is new here; people have only been doing it out of Gloucester for a few years. But when Captain Fronteiro told me the *Dorcas* needed a captain, I jumped at the opportunity."

"Is swordfishing very different from other types of fishing?" Silva asked.

"Very, very different. First of all, we don't need to go as far out to sea. For fish like cod, halibut, or mackerel, we would have gone much farther offshore, to Sable Island or the Grand Banks, and we'd be away for many weeks, if not a month. Also, Captain Fronteiro has invested in a new auxiliary motor for the *Dorcas*. It can solve a lot of problems if the winds aren't in our favor or if the weather turns on us. But the most interesting thing," Joseph continued, "is that a lot of what we do in swordfishing is adapted from the way we went whaling in the Azores."

"How many times did you go whaling in the old world?"

"Quite a few times, before I left for university in Lisbon. One time I was working on the farm in my village on Pico when I heard the firework signals go off. I ran toward the whale-watch tower and saw the flag that indicated a sperm whale. Within minutes, our entire crew had met at our *canoa*. I had to stop and catch my breath before we launched. There were eight of us. We launched our *canoa* first, before any of the others."

"And did you get one?"

"Yes, because we launched first. The unwritten rule was that whoever harpooned the whale first got to plant their flag. That's not easy to do. The *canoa* itself was over thirty feet long. It had a sail and a mast we could put up if the wind was just right, but usually the six of us rowed. We had six pulling oars for going fast over a long distance, and six paddles for making quick turns and maneuvers. Back astern, one more man was in charge of the rudder and a steering oar.

"*Canoas* were great for going after sperm whales, but you didn't want to be out in one during an unexpected squall—that was very dangerous. Fortunately, most of my whaling trips were in the summer, when the weather was grand; you could often see the peak of Pico in the distance. The skipper would be up front, serving as the striker. You could row right up to the sperm whales if you muffled the oars with leather straps. When approaching the pod, we once came right beside a big male, a fifty-footer. On that trip, our skipper struck with his first harpoon."

"How big do sperm whales grow?" Silva asked.

"The big males grow up to sixty or sixty-five feet long. The cows go up to about forty. That's a pretty big whale to go after in a *canoa*. They're toothed whales, but they only have teeth in their lower jaws. Still, that doesn't stop them from hunting giant squid." The thought of a squid's giant tentacles made Joseph feel uneasy, and he hurried on with the story. "We tied the harpoon line to the *canoa* and tired the whale out, and then we pulled ourselves up real close and the skipper used a long lance to stab it in the heart to finish it off. It only took a few tries. When sperm whales die, they float at the surface. That's how you're able to get them with *canoas*. And after you harpoon and kill it, all that's left to do is to plant your flag. Then a bigger boat goes out to tow it back in, while you row back to the harbor and celebrate with some wine or, even better, some port."

"It sounds exciting, but dangerous," Silva said.

"Very much so. There are way too many Silveiras and Silvas from our island who were lost at sea going after sperm whales, including my father. That's partly why we came to Gloucester: less peril to life and limb, in theory."

The wind was gusting and the sea continued to be a bit choppy, which made spotting swordfish more difficult. The *Dorcas* motored her way northeast through the Great South Channel, while Joseph pondered the benefits of the auxiliary engine.

* * *

Sebastian was down below in the engine room, checking in on the young engineer.

"Looks like you've got things bung up and bilge free," he said. "Great work, Tone."

Satisfied that the engineer had matters well in hand, he headed topside and climbed up onto the crosstree. He enjoyed the view from this vantage point and gazed out at the horizon for about twenty minutes. All he could see were whitecaps—less than desirable fishing conditions.

At last he decided to check in on Doc and grab a mug of coffee. He climbed down from the mast and entered the galley. "Morning, Doc."

"Good morning, friend," the cook replied. He was washing

the pots and pans from breakfast.

Sebastian drank his coffee quickly and helped himself to another cup.

"Something on your mind?" Doc asked.

"Well, it's nothing really. I've just been thinking about my family."

"That's natural when you're out at sea."

"I suppose, but recently it occurred to me that I don't have a son and Joseph doesn't have one either. Neither did Manny or John before they died."

"I guess that makes you two the last of the Silveiras," Doc said.

"Well, not exactly. There's no shortage of Silveiras in Gloucester. But it does make us the end of our father's line."

"You're both still young enough to keep trying."

"Yeah, I suppose anything can happen. Joseph was older than me when they had Winnie. But I've been thinking about my daughters too. What would happen to them if something went wrong out here?"

"Fishing is a dangerous occupation, that's for certain," the cook agreed. "I often worry about the same thing. I don't really have a good answer to that question."

Sebastian had hoped for some more direct advice. He left the empty mug on the table and walked out onto the deck.

He felt full of energy now. Rolling up his sleeves above the elbows, he climbed back up onto the crosstree. From there he had a panoramic view of Georges Bank as the sun traveled along its ellipse over the clear blue sky. The choppy ocean glimmered beneath it. *These are the days when it pays to be a swordfisherman,* Sebastian thought, as he gazed out in wonder. The only thing that could have made the day better was a glimpse of dorsal fins breaking the surface.

* * *

Joseph was still at the helm with his nephew. He had decided it was time for Silva to stop asking questions and get to work with the rest of the dory mates. "You need to get ready to toss barrels," he said. "We'll be starting to fish soon."

The *Dorcas* turned and started to make her run along the Northern Flank. Silva, Brown, Merico, and Murray prepared to throw kegs overboard. Sebastian was already in place on the crosstree, ready to spot swordfish on the surface. Joseph remained astern at the wheel box, driving the *Dorcas*. (This style of wheel faced aft, and usually Joseph would stand at the right side of the wheel house and turn the wheel from the side, so he could see where he was steering.) Domingoes had made his way to the end of the bowsprit and was lying on the pulpit with an armed harpoon.

Steadily they patrolled the surface, searching for swordfish. After several minutes they saw strange activity heading straight toward the *Dorcas*. There were creatures at the surface. As they got closer, the disturbance was revealed to be a pod of eight white-sided dolphins, traveling in single file. One dolphin, at the lead, breached completely out of the water, showing its gray top and white underbelly before diving under again. It was followed in sequence by the next dolphin and the next and the next, as though they were playing a game of Follow the Leader. As they passed the *Dorcas*, the crew watched their movements, then turned their attention back to the sea ahead, looking for their prey. All they saw were waves.

"Take the wheel for a bit, brother," Joseph said to his first mate.

He walked down to the galley and helped himself from the fresh-brewed kettle of coffee that Doc had ready. "What's for lunch today, Doc?" he asked. He saw a loaf pan with what looked like corn-bread dough, a bowl full of beans, and a bunch of turnips on the table.

"Corn bread and fava-bean soup, skipper—a classic Azorean recipe," Doc replied.

"Sounds good. Let's try to have that ready at noon, after we finish the morning run."

"You got it, skipper."

Joseph returned to the helm.

During all of that morning's run they had no luck. A few hours after lunch, the *Dorcas* turned south and ran past the Northeast Peak. Then she turned south toward Corsair Canyon. So far there had been no sign of life anywhere on Georges Bank. "We could have changed over," Joseph reminded his brother. "Looks like we just bowed the compass all day for nothing."

"Our luck will change—I know it will, brother," Sebastian insisted.

"I hope you're right. It's been a while since we've had a

broken trip."

There was no change in their luck that day. They turned southwest and patrolled the Southern Flank for the rest of the afternoon. Joseph saw no marine life at all, aside from that pod of dolphins.

* * *

Smokey Joe strolled through downtown Gloucester with his oldest daughter, Mary late that afternoon. He was sixty-five years old, with short gray hair and a round jovial face. He had a stocky build and today was dressed in a dark suit with a bowler hat.

Lately he had felt very nostalgic about his long fishing career. He had grown restless in his retirement. On idyllic summer days such as this one, he often considered taking a few more swordfishing trips. He missed the summer action.

He and his daughter walked arm in arm past the Portuguese Club and toward the Master Mariners' Association Hall above the Sterling apothecary. They passed summer roses, dahlias, and hydrangeas. The flowers made Smokey Joe think back to where he had grown up, on Pico in the Azores. The few roads on the island were lined from end to end with hydrangeas, and where there weren't hydrangeas there were plenty of wild morning glories. He remembered how deafeningly noisy it had been to walk through the countryside surrounded by the hum of insects in the fields. Now he could hear a similar din from all the city folk who descended upon Gloucester at this time of year—a similar sort of invasive pest, he thought.

What he remembered best about growing up on Pico was the ever-present view of the big green volcano that towered up from almost every vantage point. No matter where you went, whether it was down to the harbor, to Madalena on the other side of the island, or out into the farmlands and fields, you could always see the volcano up above you. He could still visualize it in his mind's eye. The only time it was absent was when it was obscured by clouds or fog.

"Tell me again about when you changed your name, Father," Mary said.

This was an old story. "Well, you see, my dear," Smokey Joe began, "I came here from the Azores when I was a lot younger than you. I was just fifteen—"

"—and you had just two coins in your pocket," she said, finishing his sentence.

"That's right, and I couldn't read or write none neither. And when I registered myself at city hall, the clerk told me nobody would be able to say my real name, Joseph Pereira, and I should go by Joseph Perry. But when I was a boy, all the girls called me Joseph the Rose. And since my favorite rose from the Azores is the misquite rose, I went with Joseph Perry Mesquita."

"You spelled it wrong," Mary teased.

"Spelling was never my strong suit," Smokey Joe said, laughing. "I worked my way up the fishing ladder. First I found room and board with Captain Silva, and then I became a dory mate on his vessels. Then, nine years later, before I became a captain, I became a citizen. And I married your mother, after working for her father."

They passed some more hydrangeas forming a neat row along one of the townhouses. Then Rosella Nunes walked by them, wearing a blue dress and a matching hat that were the same powder-blue as the hydrangeas. She carried a brown paper bag full of groceries.

Smokey Joe kept his gaze focused forward, and Mary said, "All the other men on the street turn their heads when Mrs. Nunes walks by."

"All the other men must not be as happily married as I am," Smokey Joe retorted. It was the truth; he loved his wife and family. But still he longed to go back out to sea. He missed catching swordfish.

* * *

Birdie watched Mama prepare their evening meal in the kitchen while she got ready to go out for a treat with Le. There were potatoes and parsley on the counter, and in the sink was a bowl full of water and reconstituted salted cod.

"*Bacalhau*, my favorite," Le said.

"Don't you go spoiling your appetites for dinner," Mama admonished them.

The two sisters stepped out the front door and walked to the drugstore for an ice cream. Birdie had only a few more weeks until she went off to the Eastman School of Music in Rochester, New York. Earlier this spring she had received a letter with the exciting news that she had received a scholarship there. She was excited and nervous at the same time. She had never been so far away from home before, and she wasn't sure how she would respond to it.

As they approached the drugstore, Rosella Nunes walked past them with her bag of groceries, her blue dress revealing her voluptuous contours.

"Do you think she's beautiful?" Le asked her older sister.

"I think everyone in Gloucester must think she's beautiful," Birdie said. She opened the door to the Melvin H. Perkins apothecary, and they sat at the counter and placed their orders.

"A scoop of pistachio, please," Birdie said to the fountain jerk.

"Blackberry, please," Le said.

They enjoyed their ice cream together for a spell.

"I've only got a few more weeks here," Birdie mused, "and I probably won't be back again until the holidays."

"That sounds good to me. Maybe I'll be able to read the newspaper every once in a while."

"You know you're going to miss me," Birdie said.

Le stayed silent and ate her ice cream. Then she remarked, "I don't know how you can like pistachio ice cream. No true Azorean would order pistachio. Pa always gets blackberry."

"I'm not an Azorean, I'm an American," Birdie replied.

"You sound like Pa," Le said.

* * *

Mary was in the kitchen preparing dinner with her youngest daughter.

"Does Pa catch cod?" Winnie asked.

"Yes," Mary replied, "but usually not at this time of year." She was remembering that Joseph hadn't wanted to go out on this trip. Maybe he should have changed over as he'd planned.

She returned her attention to the two-pound piece of *bacalhau* in the sink. She had soaked it overnight to reconstitute it. Now she put two large pots of water on the stove, and also a frying pan. While the water came to a boil, she chopped up four onions, minced some garlic, and fried all of it in the pan. Next she chopped up six boiling potatoes.

"Which way is this, Mama?" Winnie inquired.

"What do you mean, Winnie?"

"Le said that you know three hundred and sixty-five ways to cook cod, one for each day of the year."

"*Bacalhau*," Mary corrected her.

"To cook *bacalhau*."

"This is number two hundred and thirty-four," Mary joked. "An old recipe from the Azores." It was indeed a traditional Azorean recipe—she had learned it from friends in the community—but the number was a game she played with Winnie.

When the water came to a boil, she added the *bacalhau* to one pot and the potatoes to the other. Then she and Winnie set the table. Once the food was cooked, she drained the water from the potatoes and stirred in the onion and garlic. Then she scooped the potatoes onto a serving platter, layered the boiled *bacalhau* on top, and prepared a garnish of chopped boiled eggs, parsley, and black olives.

"Dinner's ready," she announced. "Winnie, can you gather

your sisters?"

"Okay, Mama," Winnie replied.

*Maybe he should have changed over after all,* Mary thought again. She couldn't figure out why she had become so anxious all of a sudden. Normally she was calm and stalwart—important traits for a fisherman's wife. But today she had her doubts.

\* \* \*

While the crew cleaned up after the afternoon run, Joseph joined Doc in the galley. The cook was stoking up the stove by adding coal to the embers still glowing from lunch. Once he got the fire roaring, he closed up the fire box and wiped his hands on his white apron. He took off his white hat and shook it over his head, then put it back on. Only then did he put the kettle on with some water for the captain's tea.

"Dinner tonight will be a traditional Portuguese fisherman's stew, served with sourdough bread," he told the skipper. "See, I've already started reconstituting the *bacalhau.*"

While he drank his tea, Joseph watched Doc carry out the many preparatory tasks for the stew. First he peeled the potatoes and cut the onions. Next he put the large stew pot onto the stove and added a stick of butter and some black pepper. Once the butter melted, he added the onions and cooked them down until they started to melt. Then he added water and dried peas. When it all came to a simmer, Doc added the chopped potatoes and brought the pot to a boil, and then he lowered the temperature to a simmer and covered the pot, waiting until the potatoes got tender.

Soon the stew was coming together nicely, so he added condensed milk and stirred it up, then covered it for a bit to get it back to a simmer. Next he stirred in the *bacalhau* and added a generous spoonful of lemon essence.

"How much longer until dinner is ready, Doc?" the skipper asked.

"About half an hour," Doc said. He added more butter, more salt and pepper, and then the final ingredient, chopped *linguiça,* which added spice to the hearty and creamy stew. "Just like in the Azores," he said to the skipper.

Thirty minutes later, Joseph was sitting at the table in the forecastle with the crew as Doc brought out the food, right on schedule.

"You're going to like this—*bacalhau* is one of Doc's specialties," Joseph told his nephew.

"One thing we can all agree on, whether you're Sicilian or Portuguese: we all love our *bacalhau,*" Sebastian said.

"We call it *baccalà,*" Merico said, allowing his Sicilian accent to come out. "I think it sounds a lot better in Italian."

"What about us Irish guys?" Murray asked.

"I've heard a rumor that you Irish guys like cod too," Merico replied. "But the jury is still out on whether you know how to spell it."

"I'm just glad the cod industry rebounded after that Mussolini incident, or we all would have starved to death last winter. Gorton's almost went under after your guy stole all that *bacalhau,*"

Brown said.

"Mussolini is most certainly not my guy, and I'm not Italian, I'm Sicilian," Merico said.

"What's the difference?" Sebastian asked.

"Do you consider yourself Portuguese or Azorean?" Merico countered.

"Ah, I see your point," Sebastian conceded.

"I like to think of myself as American," Joseph said.

After dinner, the men conversed over coffee and tea. Some had a cigarette or smoked a pipe.

"Did you ever go out whaling in the old world like the skipper did?" Silva asked Sebastian.

"No, I was too young. I just got to watch them, from up in the *vigia da baleia*."

Unlike Joseph, Sebastian had only a few distant memories from his native island of Pico. But though he had been too young to go out on a whaling *canoa*, he told his nephew about watching a chase from one of the whale watch towers.

"There were dozens of observation towers scattered along the coast. The one in our village was on a high cliff of black volcanic stone. The watchman, would sometimes let me come up into the *vigia* with him. One time he was looking out to sea with his binoculars, and suddenly he turned toward me and shouted with glee: '*Baleia, baleia!*' He grabbed one of the tower's rockets and lit it with his cigarette, then aimed it out the window, straight up. He let me raise a flag onto the pole at the top of the tower. That was the highlight of my month. The flag had a sperm whale on it, so everyone would know that sperm whales had been spotted. Within minutes *canoas* were being launched down the boat ramps in a desperate race. And Joseph was in the *canoa* that got there first."

After Sebastian finished his story, the other crew-members told tales of their own, while Doc cleared the table.

Then Sebastian remembered that he still had one more duty to perform that day as first mate: assigning the watches. "Choose a number, you lumpers," he said to the crew.

"Three," Brown said quickly, beating the others to it.

"All right, men, thumb on the hat," Sebastian commanded. He placed his hat upside down on the table, and each man put a thumb on the brim. Sebastian closed his eyes and randomly chose a thumb on the hat; he was careful to do so fairly. Then he opened his eyes and counted clockwise to three. "One, two, three," he said, stopping on Silva's thumb.

"You drew the first watch, greenhorn," Merico said.

"Yes. And now you need to choose the two men who will join you," Sebastian said.

"Tone and Domingoes," Silva said.

Sebastian knew that Silva would never voluntarily choose Brown or Murray.

* * *

Later that night, the crews of the many schooners of the Gloucester swordfishing fleet slept in shifts, like those on the *Dorcas*—all anchored for the night near to each other and near to the lightship *Nantucket*. They anchored close enough that they could signal for help but far enough away to maintain elbow room and a modicum of privacy.

At night the sea became completely dark underneath the surface, and many squid came out from their deep holes below. The cephalopod throngs started to meander closer to the surface to feed. Unfortunately, their bioluminescence was a give-away: the swordfish had also arrived and were waiting for them in ambush, and they fed voraciously all night. It was a veritable squid smorgasbord.

# Nantucket Sleigh Ride

> Ho! see ye not, my merry men,
> The broad and open sea?
> Bethink ye what the whaler said,
> Think of the little Indian's sled!
> The crew laughed out in glee.

*A Ballad of Sir John Franklin*, George Henry Boker

### Saturday, August 23, 1924.

J oseph had awoken early, and he had already poured himself a mug of coffee. He brought it up to the helm and watched the sunrise off in the east, while the *Dorcas* remained at anchor by the lightship near the Nantucket Shoals. He wrapped both hands around the warm tin mug and took a swig. Just then the sun broke over the black horizon like an egg. The black turned into orange, and the orange was replaced with light blue. There were a few low-hanging clouds, but other than that the conditions seemed perfect for swordfishing.

Joseph went down to the galley. "What's on the menu this morning, Doc?"

"I figured that today would be a good day to use the blueberries, before the salt air ruins them, so I'm going to do pancakes today."

Joseph poured himself some more coffee and watched as Doc got the fire going in the stove. Then he finished making the pancake batter, adding the berries at the end. Once he got a few frying pans hot, he added some butter, poured in the first batch of batter, and made dozens of pancakes.

Joseph helped him bring out the first stack to the forecastle table with some sausages, along with butter and maple syrup, and joined his crew for breakfast. By the time Doc returned with the second stack, grace had already been said and the first stack had been consumed by the skipper and his hungry crew. They helped themselves to more pancakes and sausages, and Joseph listened to the crew as he ate.

"Be careful out in the dory today, greenhorn," Murray said to Silva. "I've heard the sea serpent has been seen again this summer."

"Sea serpent?" Silva asked.

"Yes," Brown chimed in, "legend has it that it comes up to the surface every twenty-five years to feed. The last time it was seen was in 1899, by the steamer *New England*. They say it was almost fifty feet long and shaped like a snake."

"Belay your jaw tackle, Mr. Brown," Joseph said. "That's enough with the sea-serpent stories. It's time to earn your pay."

The men pushed back their chairs, thanked Doc for the grub, and set to their tasks.

Later in the morning, when they arrived at the Great South Channel, the sky was mostly clear, with occasional wisps of cirrus clouds. Joseph had been disappointed in the lack of good fortune on their first day, but, not one to be deterred, he made sure his crew was fully ready for this new day. So far, the conditions looked favorable.

There was practically no wind, and the water was almost still.

His nephew stood astern with him to get a good view of the crew. Joseph gave him some instructions on the finer points of swordfishing as the schooner ran around the southern edge of the bank toward the Southern Flank. "Sebastian will point out where to steer," he explained, gesturing toward his brother, who was high in the crosstree of the mainmast, watching for signs of swordfish.

"Are they hard to catch?" Silva inquired.

"Yes and no. They're not that intelligent, but they are hard to find."

The *Dorcas* headed toward Corsair Canyon. Joseph turned the wheel based on the signs he got from his brother. He told Silva to pay attention to the rest of his dory mates, who were ready to throw barrels and launch dories on his command.

"*Espadarte a vista!*" Domingoes shouted for the first time on the trip.

A swordfish had been spotted: Joseph could see its sickle-shaped dorsal fin and matching tail fin breaking the surface, a signature pattern for a swordfish at the surface. Sebastian pointed from the mainmast, relaying information from Domingoes so that Joseph could steer the *Dorcas* toward their prey and put Domingoes into position to strike.

That particular swordfish had hatched many years ago off the eastern coast of Florida, in the warm Caribbean currents. Ever since reaching adult size, she had followed a consistent annual migration pattern. At this time of year, she moved up the Atlantic coast as the water temperature rose and the ecosystem shifted in Georges Bank and the Grand Banks.

As the warmer Gulf Stream waters cycled up north and collided with the colder Labrador Current, the warm water and ample sunlight created the perfect environment for phytoplankton, food for very small fish. They attracted massive schools of baitfish, like herring and mackerel, and they in turn attracted apex predators like the tuna and the *Xiphias gladius*—more commonly known as the broadbill swordfish.

This one was a female in her prime breeding years. She weighed an impressive 418 pounds, heavier than almost every human being on the planet. In general, female swordfish grow larger than the males. Many of the swordfish caught in the 400- to 500-pound range are female.

As she cut across the surface, she showed her purple, gray, and opal side. With her large eye, she saw the silhouette of the *Dorcas* in her periphery but gave it no heed, dismissing it as unthreatening, much as she would do with a large whale. The only creatures she considered threats were mako sharks and killer whales, these being the only large predators who could match her speed. The *Dorcas* was clearly not a mako or an orca.

Even when the metal barb from the harpoon sank deep into her back with a burning pain, she made no association between that pain and the 53-foot schooner trailing her by about ten feet. As she tried to sound, she exerted an inordinate amount of energy but was unsuccessful, on account of the surprising new amount of drag. The harpoon slowed her down and caused the injury in her back to shock her with radiating pain, due to the barb of the lily iron tied to the rope, which was in turn tethered to the barrel.

Joseph was elated that they had struck a swordfish at last. He turned the wheel so that the *Dorcas* veered toward their quarry.

"*Um!*" Domingoes shouted, enumerating the first strike of the trip. He looked back toward the skipper and grinned.

Silva stood behind Domingoes on the deck. He held the main rope, which was connected to the fluke of the harpoon, to the hundred feet of line coiled in the tub, and to the fifty-gallon keg.

"Don't forget, you have three jobs," Sebastian called down from the crosstree. "One, make sure the rope doesn't get wrapped around Domingoes' leg. Two, throw the keg overboard upon Domingoes' command. And three, splash water on the rope in the tub."

Domingoes gave Silva the sign, and he tossed the keg overboard and splashed the rope in the tub. The dory mates waited to be dispatched to go and fetch the swordfish. Normally this would happen immediately after a swordfish was ironed, but in this case Sebastian saw another fish cutting out only fifty yards away on the starboard side.

"Get ready for another one!" Joseph yelled.

Domingoes took the next lily-iron barb and fitted it onto another ash-wood harpoon. Armed harpoon in hand, he manned the pulpit.

Sebastian pointed in the direction he wanted his brother to

steer, toward the wind in order to cut off the path of the second swordfish.

Joseph figured that the second fish was not a traveling companion of the first one but simply migrating along the same path, called by the same annual rhythm of instinct. This one had streaks of white, blue, and green on its body, and he estimated it to be 450 pounds. It had been finning out—showing its pair of fins—about fifty yards ahead of the first swordfish. Probably it was trying to warm its body in the morning after a feast of squid the night before.

The trio of Joseph, Sebastian, and Domingoes had caught many swordfish together this summer, and by now they could communicate mostly nonverbally. Sebastian provided the eyes from above as Domingoes struck at the swordfish and Joseph drove the schooner.

When they got within ten yards of the second fish, Domingoes prepared to strike. Silva was ready with the brown rope and the keg. The swordfish rode the crest of a wave directly in front of the pulpit, and Domingoes aimed the harpoon right into its flank. The lily iron entered its side near the spine. *"Dois!"* he declared, continuing to count his strikes.

The ironed swordfish thrashed in the red, billowing foam, and Silva tossed the second keg overboard. He then poured water from the draw bucket into the tub as the rope uncoiled.

Domingoes had ironed the first two swordfish of the trip, and the *Dorcas* was off to good fortune. Both pairs of dory mates were preparing to launch their dories. Sebastian told Brown and

Murray that they should launch after the white, blue, and green swordfish, the larger of the two.

"Time to earn our pay," Murray said to Brown. They launched their dory over the port rail.

Silva waited for Merico so that they could launch the other dory, and Sebastian climbed down from the crosstree to share some wisdom with his nephew.

"Joseph and I have only been swordfishing for one season," he said, "but from what we've learned, those two fish are probably not mates. We often find a pair together at the surface, keeping plenty of space between themselves."

"Will we ever find more than two together?" Silva asked.

"Rarely, but every once in a while we see three or four together. The most I've ever seen in one spot is five."

"Are they feeding on the surface?"

"Unlikely. I've never seen one feeding. I think they're just basking in the sun during a long migration, following the current. These two were harpooned cleanly, right through the back, so they should be easy to fetch. The ones you don't want to go after are the ones that get ironed in the head. They're known to go crazy when that happens. Sometimes, before they give up the ghost, they'll even attack a dory with their sword, and that's when you find out why we call them the gladiators of the sea. All the same, be careful pulling this one into the dory with your gaff. They don't really have teeth—with your glove you can handle them around the mouth, not like a shark or a bluefish—but it's still best not to get your arms or hands anywhere near the head. Many a swordfisherman comes back with scars on his arms or shoulders from a sword that turned at the last second. So be careful."

Merico joined them at the dory, his long, pointy blue collar billowing in the breeze. "Let's go, greenie," he said.

"Listen to Merico," Sebastian urged Silva. "He's been doing this for a while, in Gloucester and back in the old world, so you can learn a lot from him."

Then Merico and Silva lowered their dory over the starboard rail, ready to pursue the purple, gray, and opal swordfish.

* * *

Merico pushed the dory away from the *Dorcas* with one of the ash-wood oars.

"Now you're going to get a lesson in playing it," he told Silva. "That's what it's called when we row out to catch the fish. When we reach the barrel, we'll tie the rope onto one of the cleats on the bow and then pull the fish into the dory, if it's small enough; otherwise we'll lash it to the side. If it still has some fight, we'll whack it with this murder stick." He grabbed one of the dory's wooden clubs and rapped it on the rail for dramatic effect. "And if the swordfish decides to turn around and attack us from below, we have our armor to protect us." He tapped the club on the iron plate at their feet. "It's not just for ballast—it's also a codpiece. Ha!"

Silva laughed. "How long does it usually take to play it?"

"Oh, thirty to forty minutes on average. All that resistance from the barrel tires them out. They can't dive to get away, and most of the time they bleed out before we finish rowing to them."

A small flock of sea birds circled overhead as Merico rowed away from the *Dorcas*. They reached the barrel and could see the purple, gray, and opal swordfish listing to the side, about twenty yards away.

Merico rotated the thole pins, grasped the oars by the looms, and shipped them so they could attend to the swordfish. "Grab the rope," he told Silva.

But before Silva could do so, the swordfish darted toward them. The rope went taut, and the barrel started to spin in the water.

"See that?" Merico shouted. "See how the barrel spins like that?"

He maneuvered the dory in a straight line, heading after the barrel. The swordfish appeared to have very little life left at this point. Merico grabbed the brown line, cleaned off the green seagrass, and tied it to the bow cleat. This seemed to terrify the swordfish. It summoned up just enough animus for one last desperate fight. The dory launched forward as the rope went taut; the swordfish was pulling the boat forward, under tow. The two fishermen braced their feet against the thwarts and held on.

"This is what we call a Nantucket sleigh ride! Yeehaw!" Merico cheered. He waved his blue hat over his head like a cowboy.

The swordfish pulled them forward for at least eight seconds. Then it stopped abruptly; the fish had died. The two dory mates hauled it up into their boat, along with the barrel. Merico sounded the foghorn to signal to the *Dorcas* that they had retrieved their prey, while Silva took a drink from the jug of water they had brought with them. They started to row back to the *Dorcas,* which would move toward them upon hearing the horn.

Out on the other dory, Brown and Murray had a more uneventful time. They pursued the white, blue, and green swordfish. It was much larger than the other one, but when they arrived at their quarry, it had already expired. They hauled it into the dory and blew their foghorn.

While they rowed back to the *Dorcas,* Murray told Brown a dirty joke he had recently heard. Brown laughed hysterically. Neither one had the courage to tell a joke like that on the *Dorcas,* within earshot of the skipper or his brother, so they saved them for when they were out in their dory.

When the two dories got back, it was time to clean and store the swordfish, swab the deck, recoil all the ropes and prepare the kegs, and then eat a well-earned lunch.

* * *

Joseph sat next to his brother at the forecastle table. Doc served lunch to the crew, who were quite hungry after catching and cleaning the first two swordfish of the trip. Joseph thought his cook's chowder was his favorite dish—and with all his travels, he had tried them all.

"Now this is the right way to make chowder, a real New England chowder," the skipper told the crew. "Cream and potatoes. It's not a chowder if it has tomatoes in it. And in my opinion, the best New England chowder is a Down East chowder."

Doc agreed with him.

"Those people from New York City have no business calling that hot red mess a chowder," Sebastian said. "At best it's more like a tomato soup with clams in it."

"Have you tried the abomination that those barbarians in Rhode Island try to pass off as chowder?" Murray added.

"That's more like a clam bouillabaisse," Doc said.

"Hey, I kind of like Rhode Island clam chowder," Merico said.

"You would, Merico, you would," Brown said.

Joseph wiped his bowl clean with a piece of sourdough bread from the loaf at the center of the table.

Eventually the last crew-member finished his lunch and returned to work, but the two brothers remained at the table, and Joseph struck up a conversation he had been meaning to start for some time. "Let's talk about your future," he said.

"What's there to talk about?" Sebastian asked.

"Well, for one, isn't it time you thought about becoming the skipper of your own schooner, and then becoming a Master Mariner?"

"Those were always your goals, not mine."

"Well, what are your goals, brother?"

"When I figure that out, you'll be the second to know," Sebastian replied.

\* \* \*

Mary walked downtown after lunch. Saturday afternoon was

73

a perfect time to go grocery-shopping. The Model Market got fresh deliveries on that day, and if she waited until the afternoon, Bill, the owner, would have had more than enough time to restock the shelves.

As she walked she thought of Joseph. She remembered a recent Saturday after breakfast when he wasn't out fishing. He and the girls had gathered by the piano, and while Pa played, all the girls sang along with him. Later that morning he had spent time with Winnie. They had arranged all of her dolls and lined them up like a summer parade. He could be a taskmaster out at sea, but at home he was kind and loving with his daughters.

Soon she arrived at the market and greeted Bill at the register in the front of the store.

"Well, hello to you, Mrs. Silveira," he said cheerfully. "Is the captain out fishing?"

"That he is, Bill, for two days now," Mary said.

She went first to the meat counter. She thought about getting a chicken or a ham, but smoked shoulder would be the most practical choice to feed a family of six. Next she went to the produce section and put six oranges into her basket and a bag of apples. Then she added six Freestone Alberta peaches; they were fresh and in season at this time of year. To finish off her menu for the next few days, she needed some vegetables. She grabbed six ears of corn, three quarts of string beans, and six sweet potatoes. Lastly she picked up a medium-sized watermelon.

Bill rang her up and bagged her items. "That will be two

dollars and six cents, Mrs. Silveira."

"Thank you, Bill."

She paid him with exact change, then left the market and walked toward home, savoring the beautiful summer day. It was warm, sunny, and dry, with blue skies.

Usually the fish market had fresh haddock on Saturday. On a whim, she decided to stop in and see.

* * *

Sebastian watched from the crosstree as the *Dorcas* made the turn around the Northeast Peak and headed southwest along the Northern Flank for the afternoon run. Domingoes was cocked like a loaded gun. Sebastian could see a large, dark blue swordfish at the surface; they approached it from behind. He estimated it was over four hundred pounds.

Domingoes struck. "*Três!*" he cried. One of the dory mates threw the keg, and Silva attended to the draw bucket.

A few minutes later, Sebastian spotted another fish about fifty yards away. They lined up behind it, and Domingoes struck again. Unluckily, the blue-green swordfish had chosen that moment to fin out at the surface with both its dorsal fin and its tail fin.

"*Quatro!*" Domingoes shouted. The next barrel was tossed.

"That's a nice one. I would bet three hundred and fifty pounds at least," Sebastian called.

He continued to keep a lookout as the dory mates launched their boats. From up in the crosstree Sebastian had a wide field of vision. He watched as the two dories rowed out in opposite directions. This was his favorite part. From what he could tell, though, this round was uneventful for the two pairs of men. Neither dory had any trouble with its swordfish; they would be back on the *Dorcas* in no time. He started to do some math in his head. He estimated that these two swordfish together would weigh in at almost 750 pounds.

*Now, we are in business,* he thought. It was going to be a great trip for Domingoes, with his increased share. Sebastian squinted out at the horizon. The sun was warm on his face. Then he thought about his wife and daughters. Maybe he should consider a different career after all. Sure, the money was good, but he wasn't too old to make a change before the sea claimed him as a victim.

The foghorns sounded from the dories, breaking his train of thought, and he became alert again and climbed down from the crosstree.

\* \* \*

As the two pairs of dory mates rowed away from the *Dorcas* after their assigned swordfish, Murray asked Brown, "You see what's going on here, don't you?"

Brown shrugged as he rowed.

"Nepotism," Murray complained.

On the other dory, Merico and Silva arrived at their swordfish. The once blue-green fish had changed to a dull gray. Merico gave the younger man instructions on how to haul the dead fish into the dory.

As Sebastian had predicted, neither boat had any difficulty, and when they were both ready to return, they blew their foghorns, signaling to the *Dorcas*.

After they had returned to the schooner, the dory mates continued their work. They stowed the barrels and their gear, then cleaned and stored the swordfish in the ice room. Finally they washed up and met Doc in the forecastle, where a replenishing snack was waiting for them. The cook had prepared coffee, tea, a plate of hard tack, tobacco, and a few decks of cards.

"It's time for a mug-up, men," Doc said to the crew, raising a mug full of coffee as a toast.

"Nothing better than a mug-up after a hard afternoon of swordfishing," Merico added. "Now let's play some cards, fellas."

"You know the rules, you lumpers, it's always an open pantry during a mug-up," the cook said. "Help yourselves to any of the leftovers I put out, but don't spoil your appetites for dinner. And don't you dare touch the pot on the stove."

The men dealt out the cards and started their game.

"The smoking lamp is lit, so light up if you want," Doc added.

Those who smoked filled their pipes or rolled cigarettes and relaxed. They enjoyed themselves for a stretch with camaraderie and conversation, not to mention one-upmanship and sometimes deliberate antagonism.

"I don't know about you fellas, but I'm looking forward to the end of all these big parades," Merico complained. "First it was Gloucester's three hundredth anniversary, now it's National Defense

Day. It's becoming impossible to get around town these days."

"I kind of like all the historical celebrations," Silva admitted.

"You would, greenhorn, you would," Murray said.

"You know who loves a parade?" Brown asked. "Your guy Mussolini." He stared at Merico.

"If I've told you once, dimwit, I've told you a thousand times: Mussolini is not my guy!"

\* \* \*

Birdie sat at the table in the kitchen with her youngest sister; they were getting ready for an afternoon adventure. Mama had started to prepare for dinner, shelling fava beans in the sink.

"Bring Winnie back by six," Mama said to Birdie. "I don't want you late for dinner."

"Yes Mama." Birdie put a blue and white hat onto her little sister's head. "There, perfect."

She was proud of how intelligent Winnie was. *This one is going to become somebody someday,* she thought, *maybe a teacher.* To encourage her sister's education, she usually incorporated a history lesson into their little adventures around town. History and language were two of Birdie's favorite subjects, along with music, of course.

The girls walked down the hill to the harbor. "First we'll go see the launch of the *Protector,* and then we'll go to Stage Fort Park," Birdie said. She thought she might tell Winnie about Howard Blackburn's legendary adventure, but then changed her mind— Winnie was too young for that story. Instead she decided on stories about the park. "You know the history of Stage Fort Park, right?"

She told Winnie about how the English settlers had chosen that location to build their first homesteads, and how Tablet Rock had been a sacred site for the Native Americans for centuries before that.

They arrived at the harbor, and Birdie watched from a few feet back as Winnie joined the throng that had arrived to see the *Protector* off. "Good-bye," Winnie cried, waving.

"Say it like I taught you," Birdie called.

"*Bon voyage*," Winnie shouted. "*Bon voyage*." She continued to wave.

*Only five years old, and she already knows a little French,* Birdie thought. Winnie was reading chapter books too. *Maybe she'll grow up to be a writer,* Birdie mused. She had a bond with Winnie that was different from her relationships with her other two sisters, probably because of the marked age difference.

When Winnie had finished waving to the sailors on the *Protector*, they walked to the park and stopped in front of Tablet Rock. Birdie read aloud the words on the bronze plaque: "On this site in 1623, a company of fishermen and farmers from Dorchester England under the direction of Reverend John White founded the Massachusetts Bay Colony. From that time the fisheries, the oldest industry in the Commonwealth, have been uninterruptedly pursued from this port. Here in 1625, Governor Roger Conant, by wise diplomacy, averted bloodshed between contending factions, one led by Myles Standish of Plymouth, the other by Captain Hewes, a notable exemplification of arbitration in the beginnings of New England."

"Look at the pretty patina on the plaque," Birdie added. "That's the word for when metal turns a nice green with age."

A brief rain shower began, and Winnie looked up into the sky. "Raindrops are falling on my eyeballs," she said. Then she darted behind the big rock and reemerged a few moments later on top of it. She waved to her sister below, vanished, and came around from the other side, up the path from Half Moon Beach.

Birdie sat on a bench and allowed her little sister to explore. "Stay where I can see you," she said, and Winnie agreed. She ran around the front of Tablet Rock, causing a flock of seagulls to take wing. Then she walked over to the fort and crawled over the old cannon that were aimed out into the harbor in defense. Birdie looked out at the scenery and thought about her upcoming trip to college, and about Pa out at sea.

\* \* \*

On that Saturday afternoon, Smokey Joe joined the crowd that had gathered at the harbor to watch the steamship *Protector* launch. He read the program that was distributed to the onlookers as the *Protector* headed out on her first test run. The newly built, steam-powered ship was destined to become a vital component of the coastal defense and rescue capabilities of Cape Ann. Although this was just a test run to see how the new engine performed, she would go on to perform many other such patrols up and down the New England coast. She would be called upon to do search-and-rescue operations after hurricanes and to keep watch for rum-runners and bootleggers. If necessary, during times of war, she would even keep watch for hostile enemy vessels.

It wasn't mentioned on the pamphlet, but Smokey Joe knew that the *Protector* was fitting out—in other words, work was still being done on the interior, such as the finishing work on the living spaces. Lockers probably still needed to be installed, and there was still plumbing work to be done. But the ship was otherwise seaworthy, so it was a good idea for her to be taken out on a few trials while the last of the work was done.

After the launch, Smokey Joe walked back up the hill. He thought about how fair the weather was at this time of year, and how enjoyable it would be to go out on a swordfishing trip. It wouldn't mean completely coming out of retirement. His wife might even be agreeable to it.

He walked up the hill to the Master Mariners' Association. Smokey Joe and Captain Fronteiro had made plans to meet there. They shook hands and entered at the corner door of the building, on Main Street. Above the door was a painting of the schooner *Arethusa*.

Unlike Smokey Joe, who had been born in the Azores, Captain Fronteiro came from Sicily. There were many Sicilian-born captains in the Gloucester fleet, though there were many more Azoreans. Captain Fronteiro had short dark hair and dark eyes that matched his dark suit.

The two men walked up the stairs to the second floor. The stairwell opened into the middle of the main room; there were two smaller meeting rooms in the back. Smokey Joe glanced through the wide window overlooking both Elm Street and Main Street, then directed his gaze inward around the walls, at the chart of the Grand Banks, the portrait of Captain Blackburn, and all the photos of local schooners.

Some members came every day to the club to play bridge, rummy, or forty-five. Others came to smoke their pipes or cigars. Although gambling and drinking were strictly prohibited, there were two pool tables and plenty of tables set up for card games. Smokey Joe and Captain Fronteiro had come today to play cribbage. This was the real draw to the club, and on Saturdays it was common for many members to congregate during the afternoon for some friendly competition.

Captain Fronteiro smoked his pipe as the men traded fishing stories while they set up their cribbage boards. Today's topic was everyone's best year.

"You all remember the year of the strike, don't you?" Smokey Joe asked. "It was 1917, and because nobody would break the picket line, there was fish everywhere, just waiting to be caught. So I went out with a completely Portuguese crew. We created our own Portuguese union, and so, technically speaking, I wasn't breaking the picket line. I was just working with a different union." Some of the other members laughed, even though they had all heard this story many times before.

"I made over twelve thousand that year, in just three long trips on the *Joseph P. Mesquita*," Smokey Joe bragged.

"What's the most swordfish you've ever caught on one trip?" Captain Fronteiro asked, puffing on his pipe.

"Two hundred and five, on my last swordfishing trip."

"Wow," Captain Fronteiro said.

"Yeah, but the other boats in the fleet had already set the market and the price had dropped, so it almost ended up being a broken trip."

"Better a broken trip than a broken skipper, I always say."

"Truer words were never spoken. But enough of this talk," Smokey Joe added.

They began their game of cribbage, and Smokey Joe dealt first.

"Tell me, Joe, why do they call you Smokey Joe when no one has ever seen you smoke a cigarette, pipe, or cigar?" Captain Fronteiro asked.

"You're about to find out," Smokey Joe replied.

The initial play was uneventful. Then Captain Fronteiro counted his first hand, which added up to only six. When Smokey Joe counted his hand, the onlookers gave him encouragement, making it clear whose side they were on. "Smoke 'em, Joe!" one of them said.

Smokey Joe held a pair of threes and a pair of fours, matched with a five turned up as the starter. "Fifteen two, fifteen four, a run of three is seven, a run of three is ten, a run of three is thirteen, a run of three is sixteen, a pair is eighteen, and a pair is twenty." He tallied the score, then counted the crib, which further distanced him from his opponent.

About twenty minutes later the game was over. It had been

a most lopsided game.

"Looks like I've just been smoked," Captain Fronteiro admitted in defeat.

* * *

After the crew's well-deserved break, Joseph gave the command for the *Dorcas* to go under full sail again. They turned westward at the Great South Channel, back toward the lightship *Nantucket*, where they would drop anchor for the night.

"Sebastian, go below and let Tone know that he can shut the engine down for the rest of the evening," Joseph told his brother.

About thirty minutes later, the engineer emerged topside. He had a grease rag in one hand and in the other his big screwdriver, which he cleaned with the rag.

Doc had left a wash basin on the main deck filled with warm seawater, along with some towels and soap. The men took off their shirts and took turns cleaning up. Each man splashed water all over his head and torso, then lathered up with soap and scrubbed himself with the wash towel. Domingoes dunked his head into the basin and shook his head vigorously.

Afterward Joseph and the crew converged in the forecastle for the evening meal. Doc had prepared dinner earlier, while the crew were recoiling the ropes in the tubs and processing the afternoon catch. He was waiting for them with a pot full of smoked pork and raisins and a pot full of rice and beans.

"You can't serve enough fruit to fishermen," Doc told the crew. "I try to add in things like raisins and apples whenever I have the opportunity."

"A wise decision, Doc," the skipper said. He sat down next to his brother, and they enjoyed their dinner while the crew conversed.

"The Sox are on a hot streak," Silva said. "They've won seven of their last nine."

"I hadn't noticed," Brown said. "I've always been more of a Braves fan."

"The Braves? Ha!" Merico said mockingly. "Those clowns are over thirty games out of it, and it's almost Labor Day."

"The Red Sox are fifteen games out, in case you hadn't noticed," Brown countered.

"I thought you said *you* hadn't noticed?" Merico retorted, to the laughter of his companions. "But it's true, the Sox haven't amounted to anything since they traded away the Babe," he conceded.

"What were they thinking, trading the Babe?" Brown said.

"This area really needed that pennant back in '18. It was the last good thing that happened around here for a while, what with the Spanish Flu and the war and all," Merico said.

"That's true," Brown agreed.

*It's not very often that those two ever agree on anything,* Joseph thought.

"Who do you think will win the pennant this year?" Silva asked the older men.

Domingoes answered eagerly, "I think it might be the Giants

of New York, or maybe even the Senators of Washington. Yes, I say the winner will be the Senators of Washington."

After dinner Doc cleaned up and Joseph watched the men thumb the hat to see who would draw the first watch of the night. Then, remaining at the table, he updated his log book with the events of the day. He recounted their course and wrote down his plan for the next day. He also recorded the approximate weight and length of each of the four swordfish they had caught, their colors, and any other distinguishing characteristics.

"Purple and gray opal female, 400 pounds. White blue green female, 450 pounds. Dark blue male, 400 pounds. Blue green male, 350 pounds."

He closed the log book. All the crew had moved onto their evening duties. Joseph sat alone at the forecastle table and opened his poetry journal. He pondered the title of his next poem. *"Quatorze Espadarte"* was what he had written on the page, but he had not yet written the first stanza. His muse had not visited him.

# Linguiça and Donuts

There is no prayer like the sea,
Its grandeur lifts you up to the Creator,
Its perils send you on your knees to the Savior.

Old Fisherman's Prayer

*Sunday, August 24, 1924.*

The *Anita and Bernice L.* had left Gloucester for Georges Bank over three weeks before, on the first day of August. Her ice room was filled almost to the brim with swordfish. Two or three more days would be all they needed before they could head back with a very profitable catch.

Her captain, Albert Larsen, had been born in Norway, like quite a few of the fishermen of Gloucester. He was fishing with his uncle Charles, his cousins Alvin Selig and Hilary Conrad, and a crew of four additional men: Fritz Mann, the engineer; Peter Nelson; Joseph Targett; and Edward Proctor. Normally the captain's brother Andrew would have also been with them, but for some reason he had decided to sit this trip out, and so Hilary sailed in his place. This was Hilary's first time out on a swordfishing trip in the Gloucester fleet.

The *Anita and Bernice L.* had anchored overnight near the *Dorcas*, within sight of the lightship *Nantucket*. Both schooners awoke to the rising sun and prepared for their day of work. The sky was mostly cloudy, with a patchwork of alto stratus clouds and sun.

*　*　*

The rising sun warmed up the captain's quarters. Joseph woke up and went to help himself to a mug of coffee in the galley. He brought it up to the helm and looked out at the same patchwork of clouds that the rest of the fleet saw. After he finished his coffee, he gathered his crew.

Many of the staunchly religious captains of the Gloucester fleet, like Joseph, maintained a small altar or shrine on their schooners for use on Sundays. While it wasn't possible to conduct a proper Catholic Mass out at sea, Joseph could at least provide a place for prayer. On the *Dorcas*, the shrine was in the front of the forecastle. On Sunday morning Joseph would light a candle on the small shrine, which had a miniature version of the statue from Our Lady of Good Voyage, Mary cradling a schooner like the Christ child. All of the crew joined him. They knelt in front of the shrine, and there was a long moment of silence.

After this moment of prayer, Joseph led the crew to the forecastle table. Sunday breakfast was always a big event for the crew, a reward for a hard week of swordfishing.

"Did you make *filhós* for us?" the skipper asked the cook.

"A special surprise for the crew," Doc confirmed.

As the donuts turned golden brown in the oil, he prepared scrambled eggs, *linguiça,* and bacon. Soon the donuts were ready too, so he brought them out along with a fresh kettle of coffee.

The skipper led them in an old fisherman's prayer before they ate, and as he got close to the end of it, he paused briefly. Some of the crew looked around, thinking this was the end of the prayer, but Joseph made it clear that he was not done yet by stomping on the wooden deck.

Only after they had all said their amens did Doc serve the Sunday breakfast. The crew enjoyed some lively conversation.

"Skipper, tell me more about the word *saudade*," Silva requested.

"Ah, well," Joseph said, "I feel the same way about the Azores that Sebastian does. I miss it, but I couldn't go back. There were a lot of great things about living there, but the isolation of island living and the parochialism on each island gives you a sense of wanderlust—you start wanting to go find something better. Now here we live in a better place, with more opportunity for all of us." At this moment Doc brought out another plate of fresh donuts, and Joseph added, "Let's have ourselves some more of those *filhós*."

"*Prato do dia!*" Doc said in Portuguese, and repeated in English, "Specialty of the day."

"Now don't you all try to corrupt the lad with this talk about your old country," Murray said. "You're a Gloucesterman, Silva, born and bred, and don't you forget it."

"Murray's right," Brown agreed. "The last thing we need is for you to turn into one of those Porto Pico boys!" The crew laughed.

"This may have been the greatest Sunday breakfast at sea ever," Joseph declared.

"I could have done without the *linguiça*, but the bacon was good," Brown said, thus drawing the scorn of all the Portuguese crew-members.

"And the donuts were good too!" Merico added, to the agreement of all.

* * *

Birdie went to Sunday Mass with Mama and her sisters. She sat in her pew quietly, with perfect posture. With her diminutive height, sitting up straight was also the only way she could see what was happening during the church service. She listened to Father Martins as he gave his sermon, but her mind wandered, and instead of following along with what he preached, she said her own prayers for the return of the *Dorcas*. She did this anytime she was at our Lady of Good Voyage while Pa was away on a fishing trip.

Then Birdie's mind wandered even further. Her eyes darted to each of the different ship models marking the Stations of the Cross. She stopped at the *Mary P. Mesquita*. That was the ship that had been owned by Smokey Joe. She knew all about her sinking, and how only one man had drowned—no minor miracle given that the ship had been cut in two by an ocean liner. She recalled hearing that Alfred Brown had been sleepwalking at the time of the crash. He had told Smokey Joe earlier that night about a horrific nightmare. Later, after he finally fell asleep again, the crew reported that he got up and started sleepwalking.

Birdie thought about how lucky her family had been. Pa had had a relatively uneventful career so far, compared to skippers like Smokey Joe and her Azorean whaling ancestors. She hoped that luck would continue.

Eventually she started to hear the music again. In her peripheral vision she saw her sisters and Mama rise. She joined in with the hymn, singing along to "His eye is on the sparrow." Soon after this it was time for the collection.

"I want to do it, I want to do it," Winnie whispered, tugging on Birdie's blouse.

"Okay, okay," Birdie whispered back.

She handed Winnie some coins, and Winnie put them on the plate being passed down the pew. *Hopefully that will keep her content through communion,* Birdie thought. Winnie sometimes put up a fuss because she wasn't yet old enough for communion. It worked: Winnie sat quietly for the rest of mass, and soon after the final prayer all four sisters and Mama walked out of the church into a beautiful summer morning in Gloucester.

\* \* \*

The crew was in high spirits for the rest of the morning. They made their late-morning run at swordfish while motoring northeast along the Northern Flank. The ocean was so still, it was like a plate of blue glass.

Joseph manned the helm and watched his striker and crew put in a hard morning's work. Early into the run, Domingoes struck another swordfish. "*Cinco!*" he declared as the harpoon barb entered the back of the small purple swordfish.

Before they could launch a dory, they found another swordfish at the surface. This one was twice the size of the other, blue, gray, and purple. Its large size made it easier for Joseph to notice how the three colors blended into each other.

Domingoes stretched out far beyond the pulpit with his harpoon ready. He aimed and struck, but he missed his intended target on the back, instead striking the swordfish in the head. The barb did hold, though, and one of the dory mates threw the barrel, which spun as the desperate fish started to pull it through the water. Silva splashed water onto the rope in the tub.

"*Seis!*" Domingoes said.

"You two, go out after the larger one," Sebastian yelled down to Brown and Murray.

They prepared to launch after the larger fish, which would end up being one of the more difficult swordfish to retrieve during the trip.

Joseph continued to man the helm as Doc helped Brown and Murray to launch, and then Merico and Silva.

\* \* \*

While Merico and Silva rowed out after the smaller swordfish, Brown and Murray rowed out for three hundred yards after the other one. Eventually they arrived at their barrel and their quarry.

"So, Murray, the greenhorn gets all the smaller swordfish and we get the larger ones, and the crazy ones," Brown grumbled.

"Sounds like a cut-and-dry case of nepotism, if you ask me," Murray replied. "Literally, since the skipper is in fact his uncle."

"There it is," Murray said as they found the fish. "Easy now, there's still some life in it. They can go nuts when they've been struck in the head like this one."

As if on cue, the large swordfish turned toward the dory and dove. The men backed up and jumped upright as the swordfish made its attack from below, stabbing upward into the center of the dory. The iron plate hopped up an inch, and they heard a loud clang, like a medieval weapon being repelled by a shield. The impact drained the last bit of life from the large swordfish; it expired and floated up to the surface next to the dory.

The two men pulled the dead fish into the dory, and then Murray started rowing back to the *Dorcas*. But the boat started to take on water where the swordfish had punctured her.

"You know what to do," Murray reminded his mate as he rowed.

"Okay," Brown said. He blasted the horn, found the scoop, and started to bail the dory.

On the other dory, Silva and Merico collected the smaller purple swordfish and retrieved the barrel. Then Silva sounded the foghorn, and Merico started to row back to the *Dorcas*.

"Merico, why do we refer to the schooner as a her?" Silva asked.

"Good question, greenhorn. I've always assumed it's because ships have waists, laces, bonnets, and ribbons. Have you ever heard why most sailors refer to the ocean as a she?"

"No, why?"

"Because most of the time you love her, except during the

full moon. That's when they both go crazy!" Right as Merico delivered his punch line, a wave crashed over the stern and splashed him in the face, though it missed Silva.

"Ha!" Silva shouted, pointing at his soaked dory mate. "It looks like you offended her."

* * *

Sebastian helped both pairs of dory mates haul their quarries onto the *Dorcas*. After the men had stowed the dories and their gear, they recoiled all the ropes into the tubs, then met on the top deck to clean the fish and store them on ice.

Sebastian wasted no time. He hacked off the dorsal fin, the tail, and the two lateral fins on each fish, and also both of the swords. After cutting off the sword from the larger fish, he held it up for the crew to see how blunt it had become after its impact with the dory's iron plate. He passed it around to the crew, then tossed it onto the growing pile of swords from the fish they had caught so far on the trip. Then Sebastian sawed off the heads of the fish and tossed them over the rail.

"You there," he said to Merico, "open up that one. And you open up the smaller one," he said to Brown.

Murray and Silva stood to the side, assisting like nurses during surgery.

Merico used his knife to cut the larger swordfish from the fins down to the anus. Brown did the same with the smaller one. Merico pulled out all the organs from the larger swordfish.

"Mackerel and squid," Sebastian said as he saw the contents

of the stomach spill out onto the deck. "Hand them the slime knives and throw the offal overboard. Dinner for the mako sharks," he added as the men complied.

Merico and Brown stood ready with the slime knives. The crew all worked together to pull out the organs and other innards. They threw the offal overboard as Merico and Brown skillfully scraped the cavities with the halfmoon slime knives, removing the blood and guts.

"Get out that blood as cleanly as you can, men. The meat stores longer with no blood," Sebastian told them.

The men switched to bigger and sharper knives as they carefully cleaned the fish, and then again they threw the slimy scrapings overboard. The offal became a slurry of blood and guts in the water next to the ship.

"If the sharks haven't been attracted yet, this should call them like a dinner bell from miles away," Sebastian said.

The men rinsed out the cavities as thoroughly as possible. They used the draw buckets to flush the carcasses with water and clean the deck.

"Let's get them into the ice room," Sebastian directed.

Each pair of men carried a fish into the ice room, like medics transporting battlefield casualties. They filled each fish with chipped ice, then wrapped each one in an oilskin. The fish were packed in closely for storage in the ice until they could be brought to market.

The men returned topside to mop up the splatters of blood on the deck and to clean the knives and saw. Then they watched the show that had started in the water, as the mako sharks arrived to help with the cleanup. "Looks like the lawyers of the sea have arrived," Merico announced. The sharks thrashed on the surface as they fed on the offal. It occurred to Sebastian that the dark blue color of their backs was similar to the color commonly found in swordfish.

"For some reason you always see makos near swordfish," Sebastian told his nephew. "We often find them together. Their fates seem to be intertwined."

\* \* \*

Joseph continued to man the helm. He thought back to his memories of the Azores as he observed the crew cleaning the morning catch. He could smell the lunch that Doc was cooking in the galley.

After the crew finished their tasks, they cleaned themselves up and met Joseph in the forecastle. Doc served them a tray full of grilled ham-and-cheese sandwiches.

"I think the thing I miss most about the Azores is the cheese," Joseph said as he ate one of the sandwiches.

His brother agreed. "And the butter," Sebastian added.

"Forget the cheese and butter," Doc said, "I miss the octopus. What I wouldn't give for some fresh octopus! You just can't find it in the markets around here."

"I've never really liked octopus," the skipper admitted.

"It's true, ever since we were kids, he hasn't liked octopus, but I've always loved it," Sebastian said.

"Squid too—I've never liked squid either," Joseph said. "I'm not fond of anything with tentacles."

For the rest of the afternoon the Azores were on the skipper's mind. His home island of Pico was dominated by the massive stratovolcano named Montanha do Pico, which was not only the highest peak in the Azores but also the tallest mountain in the entire country of Portugal—the peak of the great oceanic mountain range known as the Mid Atlantic Ridge. Joseph had grown up in the shadow of that giant volcano, in a bedroom community named Calheta de Nesquim, near the whaling port Lajes do Pico. In that harbor there was a boat ramp near the church of São Sebastão that gave access to a deep channel leading out to the Atlantic. It was there that Joseph had first learned to swim. He could remember being carried out into the water by an uncle and seeing the church and the seawall as he tried to keep his head above water.

After several minutes Joseph caught himself daydreaming and snapped back to his current reality on the *Dorcas*.

\* \* \*

Mary started to work on dinner. When Pa was not out fishing, the Silveira family and some of their closest relatives would all take turns hosting a large Sunday dinner. Sometimes it would be just Pa's side of the family, including the Silvas. Sometimes it would be her side of the family, mostly Vieira de Freitas and Oliveira relations. And sometimes, on special occasions, it would be all of them together. This particular Sunday, only Mary and her daughters would be there for dinner. They would have to wait until the *Dorcas* returned for the next extended-family Sunday dinner.

Even though she was cooking for only the five of them, there was still a lot of work to do. She enlisted the help of her second-youngest. "Wash the vegetables in the sink, please, Kiddo."

Kiddo washed her hands and then rinsed off the six sweet potatoes and a quart of string beans. "Know what I like the most about sweet potatoes, Mama? The color."

Mary knew this was a reference to Kiddo's hair, which was bright red—quite uncommon for someone of Portuguese ancestry.

Winnie walked into the kitchen, and Mary said, "Both of you, time to prepare those beans."

Winnie dragged a chair across the floor to the sink, climbed up, and washed her hands before helping Kiddo. They trimmed all the beans and removed the strings.

Mary started to dredge the haddock, which she had already patted dry. She would wait and fry the fish at the last minute, right before they sat down for dinner.

"Is this what we're having for supper tonight?" Winnie asked.

"We're not having 'supper,' we're having 'dinner,'" Kiddo said.

"No, it's supper tonight," Winnie insisted.

"You're both right, we're having supper and dinner tonight," Mary said.

"Huh?" Kiddo asked. "Are we eating twice?"

"Nope, we're only eating one more time today."

Both of her daughters were confused by Mary's explanation.

"I thought supper was what you called dinner when it was on a Sunday," Kiddo said.

"Sometimes it is. It's really quite simple. Supper is the last meal of the day, and dinner is the largest meal of the day. Usually the last meal of the day is also the largest meal of the day." Mary watched her daughters' faces as they thought about her explanation.

"So tonight we're preparing a big dinner, and we had a small lunch today, so this is our biggest meal," Winnie said.

"And when we have family over for a big meal on a Sunday afternoon," Kiddo concluded, "that's called dinner, and when we eat soup later that night, that's supper."

"Now you've got it. And that's why they call it supper—supper as in soup," Mary said.

She continued to prepare dinner with her two youngest daughters, counting the number of days until Pa would come home from his swordfishing trip.

\* \* \*

On the *Dorcas*, Doc made a quick appearance topside to see the skipper. "Tonight's dinner will be served about six o'clock," he said.

"May I ask what's on the menu?"

"*Prato do dia:* beef, peas, and mashed potatoes. Nothing but the best after a hard Sunday of swordfishing."

"I thought the donuts were the specialty of the day," the skipper said.

"You got me, skipper," Doc said, laughing as he returned to

the forecastle.

The *Dorcas* started her late-afternoon run, south down Corsair Canyon and then southwest along the Southern Flank. At three o'clock, they spotted a broadbill finning out ahead of them. Sebastian signaled to Joseph at the helm. Tone kept the motor running below. Very quickly they came up behind the swordfish, gaining ground on the two fins cutting through the surface ahead.

Joseph watched from the helm as Domingoes threw his harpoon into the back of the swordfish. *"Sete!"* Domingoes exclaimed as the barb entered the strong back muscle of the large blue and purple swordfish.

The barb held fast, and Silva threw the barrel overboard as Domingoes attached the next barb to his ash-wood harpoon. Silva attended to the next rope, pouring some water into it.

"Swordfish!" Sebastian cried, spotting another fish finning out only twenty yards away. Joseph maneuvered the *Dorcas* toward a large swordfish with purple fins and iridium stripes.

They came close, then pushed past it and had to come around again to get back into position. Their antics didn't faze the big swordfish as they made their loop.

As they came around again, Domingoes threw the harpoon, striking the swordfish in the head. This was not an ideal place to land the barb, but it held. *"Oito!"* Domingoes shouted.

Silva threw the barrel overboard as the *Dorcas* came to a stop so they could launch the dories. Domingoes loaded another lily iron onto his harpoon. Joseph watched from the helm as the two pairs of dory mates rowed out after the struck swordfish.

* * *

Merico and Silva arrived at the blue and purple swordfish. They hauled it into the dory with relative ease, then blew their foghorn and rowed back to the *Dorcas* without incident.

"Don't you listen to all the older Portuguese members of the crew," Merico advised Silva. "They act like they invented swordfishing with harpoons. But back in Sicily, when I was even younger than you, we used to paddle into the Strait of Messina in small boats called *passarelle,* only a little bigger than this here dory."

"Did you go as far offshore as we are?"

"Hardly. In fact it was barely a mile offshore, on the eastern side of the island. We didn't need a motor or a sail. The current took us right to the fish, at the same time of year. The swordfish would always be following the currents, migrating like the ones we find here. We would stand up in the boat and paddle like a canoe—six men to a boat."

"Sounds like hard work."

"Not harder than this, just different," Merico said as he rowed. "We had a spotter up on a ten-foot pole, with a small crosstree for him to stand on. He would tell us where to paddle and set the cadence of the paddling. He would keep making one loud yelp, and if he wanted us to paddle faster, he would yelp faster." Merico imitated the yelping sound and rowed to its rhythm.

"How did you harpoon them?" Silva asked.

"We would paddle right up to the fish, and the striker in the

101

bow would harpoon it with a long lance. It was a different style of harpoon, longer than the ones Domingoes throws. And after we caught a bunch of them, we would paddle back. The best part was when we cooked one of them on a big bonfire on the beach and fed the whole village."

"That sounds pretty great. How do you say swordfish in Italian?"

"*Pisci spata*," Merico said.

"*Pisci spata*," Silva repeated. "It sounds better in Italian than in Portuguese."

"You bet it does," Merico said. "Everything sounds better in Italian than in Portuguese. No offense, greenhorn, I know your language is one of the romance languages, but to me it sounds like someone chewing on a bunch of Spanish words and then spitting them back out again. Ha!"

"No offense taken. It's not really my language—I didn't grow up with it."

On the other dory, Brown and Murray did not have the same luck with their swordfish. Their purple and iridium-striped fish went crazy, attacking the barrel for almost thirty minutes. It swam at it, swatted it with its sword, and eventually succeeded in destroying it. However, in doing so, it tired itself out. At last, while the fish floated motionless in a state of exhaustion, Murray lanced it skillfully, and he and Brown hauled it into their dory.

"Hey, Murray, why do we always get the crazy ones that got struck in the head?" Brown said. "At least we don't have to haul the barrel back up. At least we've got that going for us."

"Nepotism," Murray replied, right before he blew the foghorn.

\* \* \*

"Fins out!" Sebastian yelled.

He pointed to port from up in the crosstree, and Joseph steered into the new position. The swordfish was massive—over 450 pounds in Joseph's estimation. It had a unique color scheme, with a mottle of purple, blue, and gray on its back and fins.

"*Nove!*" Domingoes yelled as he harpooned it. Silva threw the barrel overboard, and Domingoes fastened another barb onto the end of the next harpoon.

It was now five o'clock. Domingoes saw the next swordfish ahead at the same instant that Sebastian called it out. It was a small one, about 250 pounds. They were already almost on top of it, and it was harder to spot due to its smaller size. But the silver, blue, and green hues on its back and fins reflected the early-evening sun.

Domingoes positioned for a challenging strike. At first Joseph thought he might miss, but at the last second the swordfish turned right into the barb. It was harpooned deeply in the back. "*Dez,*" Domingoes said.

Murray tossed the barrel overboard, and the dory mates prepared to launch under the watchful eye of Joseph at the helm.

\* \* \*

Merico and Silva rowed out after the smaller swordfish. It was still alive but pretty well spent.

"That one should be small enough for you to haul in by yourself," Merico said. "It's still alive, so be careful. First finish it off with the murder stick."

Silva grabbed the wooden club, leaned over the rail, and whacked the fish on the head. He whacked it again even harder, then once more.

"One more good whack ought to do it," Merico said.

Silva aimed carefully and put everything he had into one more carefully placed strike.

"Okay, now gaff him the way I taught you."

Silva grabbed the gaff with both hands, and with an overhead stroke drove the hook into the neck of the swordfish.

"Perfect," Merico said.

Silva hauled the fish into the dory, drank some water, and blew the foghorn.

On the other dory, Brown and Murray hauled in the larger fish, which had once been a mottle of purple, blue, and gray but had now turned a pallid gray.

"Why did I ever become a dory mate?" Brown lamented. "The days are long, the pay is low, and the lifting is heavy."

"And the life is short. Don't forget all the perils and hazards to life and limb," Murray added.

"It really is a shame the way they lose all their color when they die," Brown observed.

"What, are you turning into a poet now?"

"Yes, as a matter of fact I am. I'm dedicating my first poem to the greenhorn. What's the Portuguese word for nepotism?"

"I'm not going to say anything about it," Murray grumbled as they hauled in their fish. "There's only one word to describe it, and that word is ——!"

Brown blew the foghorn as Murray said the expletive.

*  *  *

Sebastian helped both pairs of dory mates haul the latest catch up onto the schooner. Their total was now ten swordfish for the trip so far. Sebastian hauled the smaller swordfish up to the port rail with the winch as Merico and Brown turned the Hyde windlass. The fish was hoisted up by the tail with its sword hanging over the rail. This allowed Sebastian plenty of maneuvering room as he pulled out his large fishing knife, preparing for the gruesome work that needed to be done before the fish could be stored below, wrapped in oilskins and stuffed with ice.

"Hoist it up just a little further, you lumpers," he called.

He cut its throat, so that the swordfish could bleed out completely. After a few moments, when he was confident that there was no more blood, he lowered the fish onto the deck for the rest of the processing.

As the crew completed their cleaning tasks, Sebastian thought back to a memory from the Azores. "This is a heck of a lot less gruesome than flensing a whale," he said to Silva. "That's the word for processing a whale for blubber and meat. When we did it back in the Azores, almost nothing went to waste. In the harbor in Lajes do Pico there was a flensing platform, essentially a big ramp down to the harbor with gutters for the blood. We would pull the sperm whale up onto the platform with one of the steam winches; the chain went around the tail above the flukes. Sometimes it took practically the entire village to get through the flensing. We would work for hours. First we would strip off all the black skin. We would cut off two-inch strips to be used as bait by the fishermen."

"How old were you when you flensed your first whale?" Silva asked.

"About twelve. I was too young to go out on a *canoa*. Most of the flensing was done by the men, though. Two men with big hand spades would cut a deep incision around the neck, and then they used a big cable to sever the head."

As if following his story, the dory mates hacked off the head of the swordfish they were cleaning.

"I remember hearing the gurgling of the blood as it flowed down the gutters into the sea. It was all over my legs and feet; I was painted in crimson. You had to be careful not to slip and fall into it. Next the two men would collect all the spermaceti from the case in the head. The spermaceti would get processed separately because it was a lot more valuable. Then it was time for the blubber itself. That took even more people. We would cut it into two-foot strips. Sometimes we boys got to climb up on top of the carcass to help peel off the strips with big iron hooks, and then we would haul it up to the whaling factory up the hill.

"After the blubber, it was time to butcher the meat. First we would cut out big strips of belly slab, back strips, and steaks. We ate a lot of whale meat back then. The best part was the ribs. Often we would cook them on bonfires on the beach, and then the rib bones would get ground into meal for the farmers. Last but not least, there were the teeth. They were reserved especially for the crew-members from the *canoa* that got the whale, as mementos. The teeth were precious, prized for use in the art of scrimshaw.

"After that, what was left of the carcass was towed out to sea, to be finished off by sharks. You could start to smell the blubber and spermaceti getting refined. It actually smelled good, if you can believe that. I think it was because of the fragrant *faya* wood they burned in the factory. When I was a boy, I thought it smelled like a giant chicken roasting in a wood-fired oven."

At this point the swordfish were both cleaned, and Sebastian stopped reminiscing to help the dory mates carry the two carcasses down into the ice room. Then the men cleaned up and met in the forecastle for a well-deserved mug-up.

Doc, bringing out some coffee and tea, noticed that a few of the crew were engrossed in the recent issues of *Weird Tales*. "How can you lumpers read that rubbish?" he asked.

"It's a welcome distraction from a hard job," Sebastian said. The first mate had read every issue of the publication so far. "This issue has a great cops-and-robbers story about swordfish and tuna. A couple of thugs out west at Catalina Island are using the big sportfish to smuggle opium." He held up the most recent edition of the magazine. The cover featured an Egyptian desert sunset with a sphinx and pyramids. "A couple of federal dicks catch onto their fake taxidermy scheme, and now the bust is about to go down."

"Actually, that sounds like my kind of mystery tale," the cook said. "Can I read it when you're done?"

"Oh, I've already read this one," Sebastian said. "I just like flipping through it to see what kind of jobs they're advertising." He handed the magazine to the cook and grabbed another from the pile on the table, thumbing his way through it to peruse the ads. "See, I could be a draftsman. I could study the science of fingerprinting. Ooh, look at this, I could become an electrical expert."

"If only you showed as much interest in navigation and seamanship as you did in all that pulp-fiction trash," Joseph scolded. "I would have nightmares every night if I read that Lovecraft and Poe stuff all the time."

"You already do have nightmares every night, brother," Sebastian said.

"That's true. I wish I could sleep as soundly as you do. It's as though you don't have a care in the world."

Brown was also reading one of the *Weird Tales*. "Look here, greenhorn," he said to Silva. "This one has an ad for a book that would be perfect for a young groom like you. 'Sex facts that other books don't dare discuss are plainly told in *Where Knowledge Means Happiness*.'"

"That's enough, Mr. Brown, belay your jaw tackle," Joseph said.

The men continued to read their magazines in silence. After the crew finished their mug-up, Doc cleaned up and stowed the thirteen *Weird Tales* magazines in the pantry.

* * *

Later that evening, the *Dorcas* arrived at the Nantucket Shoals, not far from the lightship. Joseph told Sebastian to tell Tone to turn off the engine. Sebastian complied, and a few minutes later Tone had the entire system shut down.

"Drop anchor!" Joseph commanded.

"Drop anchor," his brother repeated.

The men worked together to secure the *Dorcas* within view of the lightship *Nantucket*. All the sails were furled except for the riding sail, which was kept up to ensure that the bow always turned to face the wind.

Before dinner, Tone emerged from the engine room and washed the smoky grease off his face and hands so that he could join his fellow crew-members for Sunday dinner.

Joseph led the crew to the forecastle. He got a whiff of a familiar smell, which made him smile as he took his place at the table. After he had led the crew in grace, Doc served dinner. First he brought out the beef and the mashed potatoes, next the peas.

As the men ate, Merico started a conversation. "You're getting into the fishing business at the right time, Silva," he said. "I hear this Clarence Birdseye fella has a new invention that can instantly freeze fish. It's going to change everything, and we'll all be rich."

"Now I've heard everything," Doc interjected. "Who would ever want to eat frozen fish?"

"Well, I imagine you need to thaw it out first, ha!" Merico laughed.

The crew laughed with him and then finished the main course. Doc cleared away the plates and brought out the special dessert he had prepared because it was Sunday.

"Donuts for breakfast, and pudding after dinner," Silva said appreciatively. "You can keep all the frozen food—I'll stick to what Doc is serving up!"

Later in the evening, Joseph brought his log book up to the helm to write his entry for the day. He took advantage of the sunlight before it disappeared into the darkness, describing in detail all six swordfish they had caught. Then he put his pen down and watched as the sea around him blended into orange and black.

Nighttime spread over the ocean. The lightship *Nantucket* disappeared into the background, then reemerged as a beacon in the darkness. Joseph took out his poetry journal. By the light of the lantern, it was bright enough for him to write. He took out his pen and inkwell and wrote a poem to his wife about the lightship. Then his mind switched over; his thoughts now came in Portuguese. He put pen to paper, and the words in his native tongue flowed out in a steady pentameter. He deftly described the sounds of the ship as she creaked and groaned, the salty smells, and the tastes of the ocean air. He included the colors of the horizon and the lightship, fading in the last of the sunset.

From his position, Joseph could hear occasional scraps of conversation from nearby schooners. The sounds bounced over the water, though the words were indiscernible.

"It's more peaceful these days," Joseph reflected to his nephew, who was standing nearby. "Only a few years ago we would have all been sleeping with one eye open, on the watch for German U-Boats."

Merico approached them. "Good news, greenie! In addition to the history lesson the skipper is giving you, you're about to get a free journeyman's lesson in the finer points of plugging a hole in a dory." He handed the younger man a brush and a bucket filled with pitch.

As his nephew set to the task under Merico's instruction, Joseph went to his cabin and retrieved his *viola da terra*, a small twelve-stringed guitar from the Azores similar to the mandolin. He reappeared on deck and started to strum some *fado*. "Here's another free lesson about *saudade*," he said to his nephew. The sharp, quick notes twanged and skipped across the waves below, getting absorbed by the ocean.

* * *

There were about a dozen other sworders anchored for the night near the *Dorcas*. Many were also part of the Gloucester fleet. They maintained about fifty yards of space between each other. None were close enough to hear the sounds of the viola.

The nearest vessel to the *Dorcas* was the schooner *Funchal*. She had been built in Rockport in 1918. She was a bit larger than the *Dorcas* at 61 feet, and she could handle a larger crew, of fourteen. She had a sixty-horsepower, oil-fired marine engine and was owned by

William Tarvis of Provincetown. Her captain, Louis Sears, was a good friend of Joseph Silveira. They had often fished with each other in their years of running for the Boston market. It was common for two friendly skippers to anchor near each other when they were out at the same fishing grounds.

Next to the *Funchal* was the *Christie A. Cox*, under the command of Captain Antoine Brown, and next to her was the *Helen E. Murley* from New Bedford, under the command of Captain Andrew J. Kinney. Beyond her was the *Alice and Wilson,* under the command of Captain John Hall. Much like the *Dorcas* and many other ships in the fleet, the *Alice and Wilson* had found plenty of success that day catching swordfish.

The fleet retired for the night, resting up for another day of swordfishing on Georges Bank.

# Thirteen Swordfish

Nature her bounty to his mouth confined,
Gave him a sword,
But left unarmed his mind.

Oppian

*Monday, August 25, 1924.*

The eye of the storm had already formed nine days ago, 420 miles southeast of Barbados. After some minor devastation and disarray in the Caribbean, it had skirted the southeast coast of the United States for a few days, then made its way from Florida up toward the Georgia coast. At six o'clock this morning, it had reached its peak strength as a Category Four hurricane, with wind gusts in excess of 135 miles per hour. It continued to move up the coast past the Outer Banks, following a northeast track, in a direct line toward the Gloucester swordfishing fleet out at Georges Bank.

\* \* \*

The White Star Line *Arabic* was steaming ahead at full speed, at seventeen knots, powered by her twin-screw propulsion system. She was about halfway to New York by way of Halifax, after having recently crossed the Atlantic on the maiden voyage of her New York to Hamburg route. She had departed from Germany, with a stopover in Southampton, England. She was 590 feet long, weighed almost 17,000 tons and had been built in 1908. Originally she had been used as a German navy vessel, laying down minefields in shipping lanes during the Great War. Four years ago she had been purchased by the White Star Line and converted into a transatlantic ocean liner. On this trip, the *Arabic* was under the command of Captain V. W. Hickson. Most of her 616 passengers were European immigrants destined for Ellis Island, but many of her first-class passengers were well-to-do Americans returning from their summer holidays in Europe.

The Mackie family was seated at their table in the dining room of the *Arabic,* eager for breakfast. A waiter came over with a basket containing breads and pastries.

"Enjoy what you like—we're on holiday," Hugh Mackie said to his nine-year-old daughter.

"I can't decide: do I want a corn muffin or Vienna Bread?"

While his daughter contemplated, Hugh read through the breakfast menu, which was in English on the left side and in German on the right. He decided he would order poached eggs, grilled ham, and potato griddle cakes.

At the next table over, Frederick Dickens' sons had not been nearly as picky when it came to eating. The waiter cleared away the remains of their cantaloupes and muffins. The Dickenses were returning from their summer holiday in England, and their two boys were still hungry for more.

Back at the Mackie table, the waiter came around with the fruit tray, and Hugh's daughter found herself in another dilemma. "Should I have a banana or some grapefruit?" she mused.

By the time she had made up her mind, the Dickens boys had

already cleaned their plates and asked for some bread, mustard, and deli meat—they were still hungry.

* * *

Joseph met the morning at the helm of the *Dorcas* with a mug of coffee. He observed the mackerel sky at sunrise. The coffee was welcome, making him more alert. Later he met his crew in the forecastle, and they fueled up with a hearty breakfast of oatmeal, cinnamon, and reconstituted dried apples. Afterward they departed the Nantucket Shoals and made their way toward the bank.

As they arrived at the Great South Channel, they saw a small pod of right whales congregating at the glassy sea surface.

"*Baleia, baleia a vista!*" Domingoes shouted joyfully. Whales, along with dolphins and porpoises, were a sign of good fortune.

Joseph heard the familiar breathing sounds from the three whales' blowholes as their spray shot upward, one after the other. When the *Dorcas* got closer, the whales decided it was time for them to move on. The two smaller calves dove first, followed by their much larger mother. She finished her dive with her signature move, a flick of her fluked tail.

Joseph steered the *Dorcas* into position for the late-morning run. In the warm August conditions, swordfish tended to bask in solitude at the surface between nine and noon. They tended to swim with the current, traveling in single file with at least fifty yards between each one.

Today Joseph's plan was to approach the bank from the south and follow the current as it flowed northward along the eastern ledge, then turn north past Corsair Canyon toward the Northeast Peak of Georges Bank. Domingoes was out on the pulpit as they searched for signs of the gladiators of the sea. They searched all morning.

Joseph was disappointed that they did not see a single swordfish during the run, especially after the favorable augury of the whales. Morning was usually the most prolific swordfishing time of the day. He handed the helm over to his brother and went down to meet Doc in the galley for another mug of fresh coffee.

* * *

The New Bedford whaling bark *Wanderer* had been built forty-six years ago at the Holmes shipyard in Mattapoisett. She was the last wooden whaling ship remaining from the fabled New Bedford fleet, and had recently been featured in the film *Down to the Sea in Ships*. She was 116 feet long and square-rigged, a classic design for a whaling bark. This was to be her swansong, her final trip down to the South Atlantic whaling grounds. Her crew of fifteen worked under the command of Captain Antone Edwards.

"Where in creation is Tom?" the third mate Conceiçao asked as they got ready to launch. "He's always topside with us when we depart on a voyage. This is totally unlike him. Tom, where are you?"

"Mystery solved," the first mate Gomes said. He pointed at the cat. "There he is, over there, still on the dock. Looks like our lovable mascot has decided to swallow the anchor."

"The bilge rats will be pleased," Captain Edwards said as they departed. At ten in the morning, the *Wanderer* was towed out of New

Bedford's pier three. When they were under their own volition, Captain Edwards instructed his crew on their sail plan. "Hoist the mainsail," he commanded.

"Aye, skipper," Gomes said. He was assisted by the third mate.

"Hoist the jumbo," the skipper directed.

"Aye, skipper," replied the second mate, Freitas.

The experienced whaling skipper continued to guide his crew as the *Wanderer* sailed toward the South Atlantic whaling waters. Her figurehead, a six-foot gilded eagle, gleamed in the morning sun, which glowed like a nimbus, diffused by the mackerel sky filled with puffy cirrocumulus clouds.

* * *

When Joseph reached the galley, Doc was stoking the coals in the stove. Joseph watched as the cook prepared rissoles stuffed with leftovers from the night before. He started by rolling out small handfuls of dough, then stuffed each with some filling and pressed them into halfmoon shapes. He sealed the edges with a fork and started to fry the pies in a pan on the stove.

Later, at noon, Joseph and his crew met at the forecastle table, and the cook served them dozens of these stuffed fried pies.

"The rissoles are golden," Merico said admiringly.

"Perfectly browned," Murray said.

"Delicious," Brown added.

"That's the second time on this trip that the three of you have agreed on something," Joseph said. "That's even more uncanny than those stories in *Weird Tales*!"

"Tone, how's the new motor been running?" Sebastian asked.

"So far, so good. They really know how to make these Sterling Fisherman engines."

"Sebastian," Joseph said, "you should focus on becoming a Master Mariner instead of worrying about the new technology. Let Mr. Rose take care of the motor."

"You've got it all wrong, brother," Sebastian said. "Life is all about the new technology now. Imagine the things we can do, the different places we can go!"

Wanderlust was a common trait of the Azoreans, and Joseph knew it was in Sebastian's blood. "Men with wisdom from experience, these are the men who weather the storm," he said. He did not share his brother's wanderlust, or his interest in modernity.

"Yes, but imagine those same men with mastery of technology as well," Sebastian said.

They were falling into the familiar circular argument that neither of them ever won. Joseph decided it was time to get back to work.

Shortly after they had all returned to their positions topside, Sebastian spotted a swordfish at the surface. It was an unusual time of day to spot a swordfish at this time of year, but he was always glad to find one, and especially now, since they had struck out in the morning run.

"*Onze!*" Domingoes yelled, making the strike.

The swordfish turned into the wind, showing its blue side, dark blue fins, and light blue stripes; it had been harpooned in the lower back. One of the dory mates threw the barrel overboard, while Silva splashed water onto the rope in the tub.

Joseph judged that the swordfish might weigh about 300 pounds. He also guessed that it was a male: the medium-sized ones tended to be male, while the gargantuan ones were usually female. He wondered why, like so many other swordfish they encountered, this one had been lethargic, seeming uninterested in them. *Might it be conserving energy for a long journey? Had it fed well the night before on squid, down in the depths below, in an overnight feeding frenzy? Why didn't the fish get spooked by the ship's engine?* He could only assume that the swordfish did not recognize the din of the modern machine as a threat. So much more to the fishermen's advantage—and another reason for Joseph to brush up on the new technology when he got back home.

"Finning out!" Sebastian yelled from up in the crosstree, pointing to another swordfish off the starboard side.

Like clockwork, Joseph drove the *Dorcas* and they motored toward the brown and gray fish.

"*Doze!*" Domingoes said as he threw the harpoon.

The barb entered the back of the medium-sized swordfish. Joseph estimated that its weight was 350 pounds.

* * *

Merico and Silva launched first, after the smaller swordfish. Out on the horizon there was a commotion of gulls, scrounging what they could from the destruction left by a school of bluefish attacking an even larger school of baitfish. The dory mates passed this fracas on the way to their barrel. The ocean boiled with bluefish and bait. Another seagull attacked the surface just off the bow of the dory, feeding on the edge of the commotion.

"Look at that, a Portuguese chicken. Ha!" Merico joked.

"I hope I'm never so destitute that I have to eat a seagull, but I guess people did what they had to during the pandemic and the war," Silva said.

"Well, I'd rather catch a Portuguese chicken than catch the Spanish Flu," Merico said.

"I guess that's true," the younger man agreed.

They arrived at the barrel tethered to the smaller blue fish. "Why does the color fade like that?" Silva asked.

"I don't know. Once they die, they lose all their color. When it's this dull, you know it's been dead for a while. Come to think of it, that's also true for humans," Merico said.

The two men hauled in their swordfish.

Out on the other dory, Brown and Murray rowed toward the bigger, brown and gray swordfish. It floated at the surface about thirty yards away from the *Dorcas*. The fish listed over onto its side, appearing lifeless, but it still had some of its brown and gray color.

"We're not safe until we get the rope onto the tail," Murray said as he looped the knot.

Both men pulled with everything they had to hoist the fish up over the rail. The fish convulsed.

"Looks like this one still has some life in it," Brown

observed.

Murray aimed the small wooden lance and drove it through the fish's ear hole into its brain, which killed the swordfish instantly. They hauled it up onto the dory along with the barrel, and Brown sounded the foghorn. Then they rowed back to the *Dorcas,* which set out to intercept them and the other dory. Although nothing was said, there was only one word on both men's minds.

\* \* \*

Smokey Joe walked down Portuguese Hill, beginning his afternoon stroll through Gloucester. He passed through the city center and once again saw signs everywhere for National Defense Day, which was only two weeks away. Arriving at the harbor, he watched the returning fishermen unload their catches. The sight made a familiar thought return to his mind.

*You ought to come out of retirement,* he told himself. *Not completely, but what if you invested in a small sworder? You could hire Arthur D. Story to build it for you, the way you did the first time you bought a schooner. And you could go on summer swordfishing trips, when the weather is fair like it is today. You could easily find another, younger, up-and-coming skipper to take over for you when it came time to change over.*

As he watched the fishermen work, he thought back nostalgically to his younger days in the Azores. He remembered making the decision to move to America. He had stood on the stern of the boat looking backward as it embarked from Porto Pico on a warm, hazy day; the giant cone of the volcano was barely visible through the low clouds. As they steamed away, the mountain seemed

121

to dissolve into the distant mist.

He thought back to the beginning of his career as a fisherman in Gloucester. He had assumed his first command in 1892—a beautiful 57-foot schooner named the *Abby A. Snow*. Over the next year, the Portuguese fishing community had boomed, and his own success grew with it. That was the year they had all come together as a community to build the original wooden version of Our Lady of Good Voyage. Smokey Joe remembered being there for the opening of the church, with more than two hundred families from Portuguese Hill.

Five years later, he had commissioned his first schooner. He bought the *Mary P. Mesquita* from Arthur D. Story, signing the contract for the 65-foot schooner by making an etching on a piece of wood because he didn't know how to read or write.

Smokey Joe walked back up the hill toward his family and his home, feeling pride in his achievements. *All I would need is a good striker and a small, agile sworder, and I could be back in business,* he thought. He would also need a good cook and, most importantly, a skilled engineer, because he didn't understand how motors worked—and without a motor, launching a swordfishing schooner wasn't viable these days.

\* \* \*

Joseph watched from the helm as his brother and the crew used the windlass and halyards to pull the larger swordfish up onto the deck, where it could be cleaned. Sebastian tied the fluke line to the tail, and Domingoes hauled on the throat halyard near the main mast. Merico in turn hauled on one of the peak halyards astern. It was slow going, but the combination of their strength, technology, and determination helped them heave the large swordfish onto the *Dorcas*.

The crew worked under Sebastian's supervision to clean and store the two swordfish as they had done many times before. Then the crew all returned to their positions to continue fishing.

But that was the last sign of swordfish they saw until they made the turn and got ready for the afternoon run down the other side of the bank, along the Northern Flank. Around four o'clock, Sebastian spotted their next swordfish, about a hundred yards off the port side. They maneuvered their way behind the massive purple swordfish. It was a goliath, clearly a female.

"*Treze!*" Domingoes yelled as he made the strike.

This was when Joseph's triskaidekaphobia set in. He was a fisherman and, like most men of the sea, prone to superstition, but Joseph's fear of the number thirteen ran deeper. On this trip they had struck thirteen swordfish in a row without missing. He had never experienced such a perfect start to a swordfishing trip, but now he felt very uncomfortable.

Merico threw the barrel overboard, and Silva doused the rope. Shortly thereafter, Sebastian spotted another pair of fins, about fifty yards ahead. Joseph maneuvered the *Dorcas* into position, and Domingoes prepared to strike with the harpoon. This swordfish was practically a twin of the other, perhaps even a little larger.

"*Merda!*" Domingoes exclaimed after lunging forward with

his throw: he had missed, for the first time on that voyage. The massive purple swordfish had turned to the right at the last second.

"I'll let that one slide, Mr. Nunes," the skipper told the striker, referring to his profanity. "What happened?"

"I made eye contact," the striker replied.

Old-timers swore that it was impossible to strike a swordfish or a whale after you had made eye contact with it.

That was the last broadbill they saw that day. The mammoth purple fish sounded deeply, reaching safety, and Joseph realized it was unlikely that they would find another one in the area.

They launched one pair of dory mates to go after the giant purple beast, which was by far the largest swordfish they had struck so far.

"Why do *we* have to go out for this one?" Brown complained to Murray, as they prepared to row out.

"You heard what Sebastian said: this one is yours," Merico responded. "We'll go out after the next one, you can be sure about that."

"I guess not all of us are fortunate enough to be paired up with the skipper's nephew. Anyway, it takes real men to go after the really big fish."

"You really are a regular Jonah!" Merico shouted.

"Why, you stupid Sicilian piece of ——!"

"Language!" Joseph called, tapping his foot loudly on the deck.

"Shinola," Brown said, correcting himself to avoid the ire of the skipper. He knew quite well that Joseph did not tolerate swearing on the *Dorcas*.

* * *

Brown and Murray rowed out after the swordfish, a massive mound of fading purple. It floated lifelessly in the sea.

"There's no way," Murray said. "We won't be able to get that monster into the dory."

"It's too big to even lash to the side," Brown agreed. "It would capsize us. Looks like we'll have to tow it."

"Yup, and you know what that means. You're rowing!"

They tied a line around the fish's tail and sounded the foghorn, and then Brown slowly rowed back to the *Dorcas*.

"I don't know about you, but I'm not going to take all that bull with the greenhorn anymore," Brown said.

"Yeah, and what do you propose we do about it?" Murray asked.

"Well, I suppose physical violence is out of the question. The skipper and his brother would throw us overboard."

"You got that right. And anyway, I wouldn't want to mess with that Domingoes fella," Murray said. "We both know how loyal he is to the skipper."

"That's true. He would pound us for certain."

"So it's settled—psychological torture it is. Any ideas?"

"We could throw some of his stuff overboard," Brown suggested.

"That's cold, even for you."

"I suppose. Maybe we could shortchange his bunk?"

"We share the bunks, you dimwit."

"Oh, yeah, good point." Brown paused to think. "Well, what ideas do you have?"

"How about the old shark-liver-oil-in-the-foot-locker treatment?" Murray offered.

"Now you're thinking. That will show him," Brown said.

While they continued to plot, some mako sharks showed up near their dory. But the *Dorcas* reached them before any of the sharks worked up the courage to take a bite.

\* \* \*

Sebastian had overheard some of this plotting as the dory approached the *Dorcas*. His blood boiled at first, but then he took a few deep breaths and regained his composure. He kept his cool while they processed the swordfish and cleaned up, and then Sebastian privately approached Brown and Murray.

"Listen," he began, "I heard you two scheming as we pulled your dory back up. You need to lay off the kid. He's working his tail off."

"Oh, cut it out," snapped Brown. "We can all see what's going on here: you keep giving him and Merico the easy swordfish because he's your nephew. It's nepotism."

"No, it's not, you dimwit," Sebastian said.

"Why does everyone keep calling me a dimwit?" Brown asked.

"Actually it's text-book nepotism, Sebastian, because he is

your nephew," Murray said. "That's what the word means."

"Stop it, both of you. Don't you remember what it was like when you were starting out as a journeyman? We should all be helping to ease rookies into the job. This is part of the dory mate's code. We all need to work together, and we need to share everything. You never know when things could get ugly out here. If you don't live by the code, you'll get what you deserve." Angrily Sebastian listed some of the many things that could go wrong. "One of you could swamp a dory. You could get impaled by a swordfish. You could get dragged overboard by a rope tangled on your foot. We could run into the rocks. You could get food poisoning or frostbite. We could get sunk by a U-Boat or cut in half by a cruise liner. We could run afoul of a summer gale. And besides, it's a small community back in Gloucester. If word gets out that you two broke the dory mate's code, it will be hard for you to find work in the fleet, especially among the Portuguese captains."

"Your point is well taken," Murray said reluctantly. "We'll follow the code from this point forward."

"Agreed," Brown said.

"Good. From now on I expect you both to belay your jaw tackle about Silva."

Sebastian's intervention apparently worked; it seemed that Brown and Murray felt sufficiently shamed to stop complaining. Sebastian hoped that would be the end of the matter.

* * *

Joseph's superstitious streak was getting the better of him.

He remembered his uneasy feeling as he had walked down the hill on Thursday. To be safe, he checked the barometer and was reassured to see a normal pressure reading. As an extra precaution, he recalibrated the barometer.

Then, while the crew was taking a break in the forecastle, Joseph saw another schooner fishing in the distance. "Sebastian, go get the binoculars," he said.

They both took turns trying to make out the name on the other schooner. After a few minutes Joseph exclaimed, "*Funchal!*" The name put a big smile on both of their faces, and they motored toward the other schooner.

"Mr. Merico and Mr. Silva, get ready at the starboard side. Mr. Brown and Mr. Murray, make ready on the port side," Joseph commanded. "Sebastian, when I give the signal, have Mr. Rose kill the engine. And you two on the portside, be ready with poles in case we drift too close."

When both schooners were within earshot of each other, Joseph called out to the captain of the *Funchal*. "Ahoy!"

"Ahoy there," Captain Sears replied. "You're pretty skilled with that auxiliary engine."

"You know me, I prefer the old ways," Joseph said. "How has the fishing been?"

"We've had pretty good luck with the swordfish. How has it been with you?"

"We're at thirteen, and we've only been out since Thursday. How many have you caught?"

"You're not going to believe this, but we're also at thirteen," Captain Sears replied.

"That's uncanny," Joseph muttered. He felt very uneasy about this coincidence.

* * *

Birdie walked down the hill with Mama. They were heading to Main Street to run some afternoon errands. After a little while they passed the dress factory where Mama used to work, near the Gorton-Pew Fisheries Company. It was just after five o'clock, and all the workers were leaving the factory, mostly women wearing blue aprons.

From there Birdie and her mother walked up Main Street, past Blackburn's Tavern. Captain Blackburn was standing out front, greeting patrons as they entered his establishment. He had short gray hair and a long waxed mustache, and he wore gray houndstooth wool pants with a black vest, tie, and cap, and a matching long-tailed coat. The sign above his head read simply "Howard Blackburn" in gold letters. Through the big window in front, Birdie could see the mahogany bar and a painting of Captain Blackburn in a dory during the storm on Burgeo Bank.

She knew all about this tavern; she had read about it in the local newspaper, though she had never personally been a patron. It was not an establishment Pa approved of. Nowadays the tavern did a steady, reputable business selling a product known as "near beer," which had a low enough alcohol level to be marketed as a soft drink. Earlier that year, the tavern had been operating as a blind tiger, but in March it had been raided by a pair of prohibition agents, who confiscated twelve gallons of liquor. In April, Captain Blackburn had pled guilty and paid a fifty-dollar fine. It took months for him to get his soft-drink license restored by the city of Gloucester, but when he did, his customers came right back for "near beer" after a shift in one of the city's many factories or a hard trip at sea. Captain Blackburn never again ventured into bootlegging; he had learned his lesson.

"Hello, Captain Blackburn," Birdie said as she passed him.

"Hello, Mrs. Silveira, and hello, Birdie," Captain Blackburn replied with a tip of his cap; he managed dexterously with the nubs on his hand where his fingers used to be.

After they finished their errands, the two women turned around and walked home. They passed the Gordon's Olympia movie house on Main Street, and Birdie spotted a poster on the marquis for the newest feature. "Abraham Lincoln," she read. "The boy who became a President. That movie looks interesting. You should go see it with Pa after he gets back."

"Wouldn't that be nice," Mama replied. "Pa does like historical films, and it should still be playing when he gets back home."

Soon they passed Our Lady of Good Voyage as they made their way up Portuguese Hill. Mama had a big smile on her face. "Only nine more days until he comes home," she said as they arrived at their front door.

* * *

The men were down below in the *Dorcas,* storing the final

swordfish catch of the day in the ice room. Packed among its giant blocks of ice and boxes full of oilskins were thirteen swordfish.

"An unlucky number for certain," Sebastian said, "but the way Domingoes has been striking, we should continue our luck tomorrow."

"Thirteen may be unlucky, but the *Funchal* also has thirteen, so don't the two thirteens cancel each other out?" Merico asked.

The crew laughed. They were in high spirits after meeting up with a friendly vessel, especially since the *Funchal* and the *Dorcas* had some history together.

"Break off enough ice from that block to fill this cavity," Sebastian instructed his nephew.

They packed the cavity of the thirteenth swordfish with big chunks of ice, then wrapped it up in two oilskins, much like the ones that they themselves wore to stay dry in foul weather. The oilskins were equally good at keeping water out and cold in.

After shutting the ice room securely, they cleaned themselves up with a bucket of sea water.

"And now let's sit down for dinner!" Sebastian said with a smile.

They made their way to the main cabin to see what Doc had prepared for the evening meal.

"Time to give Domingoes a hard time about the one he missed," Murray remarked.

The entire crew was at the forecastle table when Doc started to serve. Today it was *bacalhau* and potatoes. After Joseph led them in saying grace, Doc passed around the serving bowls. The crew was quiet. Nobody talked about the obvious until Domingoes broke the silence.

"*Treze espadarte!*" he exclaimed.

"Does *espadarte* mean swordfish?" Silva asked Sebastian. He confirmed his suspicion.

"I'll tell you what's really bad luck," Murray said as he turned to Silva. "Talking about either pigs or priests when you're on a fishing boat. That's bad news."

"But wait a minute," Merico said. "Didn't you just talk about both, by saying that?"

Murray's smile disappeared.

After the meal the dory mates turned their attention to their evening chores, and soon the *Dorcas* arrived at the shoals, where they dropped anchor.

Sebastian watched pensively as the sun set in the west. He could hear the straining of the anchor cable as the *Dorcas* undulated back and forth with the waves. Domingoes was standing nearby, leaning over a rail while he worked on a piece of scrimshaw. Sebastian was close enough to see that it was a lifelike etching of the striker's wife, Rosella. *Domingoes certainly has some artistic talent,* he thought. He remembered the first piece of scrimshaw Domingoes had completed on the trip, also on a whale tooth—a detailed engraving of the *Dorcas* with the lightship *Nantucket* in the distance, a scene much like where they were right now.

Sebastian thought about how much he missed his wife, Bella,

and his daughters, Olga and Alice. "Domingoes," he said, "when are you and Rosella going to have a family?"

"Pretty soon, I would expect. There's certainly been no shortage of trying."

"I hope you have many sons."

"You and me both! Why all this talk of family all of a sudden?"

"No reason in particular. I just think family is important."

"It sure is," the striker agreed.

Sebastian listened to the scratching sounds of metal on ivory as Domingoes continued to scrimshander, and watched the sun disappear over the western horizon.

* * *

*Only nine more days,* Mary told herself as she prepared for bed. First she would read one of the poems that Joseph had written for her. Tonight she chose the one about the cow, the goat, and the *adega* on the Azorean country road. She loved the vivid imagery in that one. Then, after feeling a little more connected to her husband, she reconnected with the Lord through prayer. Every night she prayed to the Rosary. She always wore her Rosary beads. She prayed for her husband and for Sebastian, Joseph Silva, and the rest of the crew of the *Dorcas*.

Beginning the ritual, she grasped the crucifix and said an Apostle's Creed. Then, holding the first bead, she said an Our Father. For each of the next three beads she said a Hail Mary. On the fourth bead she said a Glory Be. Then she began the first of three decades as she made her way around the loop.

Mary was very much a traditionalist. She believed in preserving the old ways, including the Azorean ones, especially those relating to food. She also believed in Catholic rituals. Both Mary and her husband were devout Catholics and were determined to pass their beliefs along to their children. The only time Joseph missed church was when he was out fishing. Mary never missed a mass. She often went during the week too, and she was an active member of the church community. She spent a significant amount of her time working in the kitchen of the Portuguese Club across from the church. Prayer was also a daily ingredient in her devoutness.

Tonight she finished her prayers to the Rosary and then thought again as she drifted off to sleep, *Only nine more days.*

* * *

At the end of the evening, Joseph saw the *Helen E. Murley* anchoring nearby, and next to her the *Mary H.* from New Bedford. They were close enough that he could make out their names before the sun set. He wasn't familiar with the *Mary H.* and made a point of entering the name into his log book. Then he noted the course they had followed and wrote down every other ship they had encountered that day, as well as a description of each of the three swordfish they had caught and the one they had missed.

Joseph stored the log book in his locker in the captain's quarters, along with his poetry journal. He climbed into his bunk to get some sleep while his younger brother took the first nighttime shift topside.

The fog of Joseph's conscious thought dissipated. His mind delved below the surface, and he dreamed vividly. He was naked, chained in leggings like Houdini. He knelt on the pulpit. His schooner was covered in ice from stem to stern. The ocean was coated in a sheet of crystallized ice all around. He could hear something sinister reverberating deep under the ice, like a loud, muffled hammer strike. It got louder, much louder. The sound stuttered in eight resounding strikes, followed by a brief pause. He could triangulate the source of the sound—it was out in front of the schooner, under the ice. During the next sequence of eight strikes, a crack formed in the ice and started to spiderweb as it spread toward him. On the eighth strike, the ice shattered. A giant orange tentacle shot through the hole and grappled one of his iron manacles, pulling Joseph overboard, down into the icy hole. He woke up right before he submerged, in a cold sweat.

# The August Gale

Like a red morn, that ever yet betoken'd
Wreck to the seaman, tempest to the field,
Sorrows to shepherds, woe unto the birds,
Gusts and foul flaws to herdmen and to herds.

*Venus and Adonis,* William Shakespeare

### Tuesday, August 26, 1924.

There was no way that any of the skippers in the Gloucester fleet could have known what was about to hit them. They had no reason to believe it was anything other than an ordinary summer gale. Sometimes storms moved up the coast faster than information could flow by telegraph, and there was not yet a reliable means for ship-to-shore communication. The entire Gloucester fleet kept their weather eyes open and checked their barometers regularly, and that was the best they could do.

The approaching deadly tempest was now a powerful Category Three hurricane, with wind gusts of more than 120 miles per hour. The eye of the storm was only a few hundred miles southwest of Georges Bank, advancing northward in a line toward Nova Scotia. The outer bands of the hurricane were getting dangerously close to Georges Bank, where many of the schooners from the Gloucester swordfishing fleet were about to start their day of fishing.

\* \* \*

Joseph met the morning at the helm, while the *Dorcas* was

137

still at anchor near the Nantucket Shoals. The sun rose red over Georges Bank, creating a diffused ruby glow like a giant fiery half-nimbus across the horizon. Joseph knew very well the old wisdom of the Gospel verse, which he recited aloud: "When it is evening, ye say, it will be fair weather, for the sky is red; and in the morning, it will be foul weather today, for the sky is red and lowering." He knew that when you saw a red glow in the morning, it meant a storm was coming.

Joseph had already experienced six different tropical storms, all of them while he lived in Gloucester; it was a very rare event for a hurricane to hit the Azores. He had missed the San Ciriaco hurricane, one of the most devastating storms and the longest-lasting Atlantic hurricane of all time. That storm had made landfall in the Azores exactly twenty-five years before to the day, on August 26, 1899. Joseph had immigrated to the United States six years prior, but he had heard all about it from other Azoreans who had since come to Gloucester. San Ciriaco had wreaked havoc in the Caribbean and on the southeast coast of the United States, from Florida to the Carolinas, before taking an extremely unusual turn eastward, gaining strength before making landfall in the Azores.

The winds today were getting noticeably stronger. Joseph could feel the gusts on his face as it blew pugnaciously. He had already given his crew the order to put up the sails, readying the *Dorcas* for their morning trip from the Nantucket Shoals to the Great South Channel. After their chance meeting with the *Funchal* last evening and the eerie news that each schooner had caught thirteen swordfish, coupled with the uneasy feeling that Joseph had experienced at the onset of the trip and the portent of this coming gale, he decided yet again to check the barometer. This time it was clear that the pressure had changed—and that was what Joseph had feared.

"The glass is down," he said to his brother.

"Yes, it certainly appears that way," Sebastian replied, barely audible over the blowing wind.

Tone was topside with the skipper. With one hand he held onto his fiddler hat, while with the other he grasped the big screwdriver tucked into his front pocket.

"Nothing to be nervous about, Mr. Rose," the skipper reassured him, "but there looks to be a strong storm coming, so it's probably best for you to get that engine started. And while you're down there, secure all the equipment and the barrels. We want to be prepared for the oncoming weather in case it gets rough."

Securing all the heavy items near the center of the ship was a good way to adjust the trim. Balancing the weight had the effect of creating more ballast.

Doc also made an appearance topside and received similar instructions from the skipper. "Stow all the supplies and the cooking gear, and the table and chairs," Joseph said. "And all the barrels and crates in the pantry. And make sure the lanterns and kerosene are handy, and the knives." Doc hurried below, and Sebastian joined his brother at the helm.

Joseph was agitated about the latest reading of his aneroid

barometer. He had seen it play tricks before, but this time he had carefully set the manual hand at the first hint of a pressure change, calibrating the device. Now any noticeable drop in pressure was a huge cause for concern.

He and Sebastian had a brief huddle to decide what to do next, and then Joseph said, "All hands on deck. The best thing to do is head toward deeper water under shortened sail."

The two brothers agreed that if the barometer dropped any further, they would set the manual hand again and then batten down the ship's hatches if necessary. Keeping only a riding sail rigged was a classic plan for sailing through a storm.

As usual, Joseph guided the *Dorcas* while Sebastian guided the crew. "All right, men," he said, yelling above the noise of the oncoming storm, "we've decided to head straight into it. We'll go under shortened sail to keep us as stable as possible. Tone, keep that motor running. We're going to need it!"

The wind rippled and blew ever louder as the crew set to their appointed tasks. Brown and Murray went to the main mast, doused the main sail, and secured the boom and gaff. Domingoes and Merico went to the foremast and did the same with the foresail. They finished first, so they went forward to the bow to take down the flying jib and the forestaysail. Brown and Murray soon joined them and doused the jumbo, which flew ahead of the foremast. The men left the riding sail up at the top between the two masts.

The crew then stowed the sails and secured the rigging, and waited with Sebastian for the signal from Joseph to put on their foul-weather gear.

Doc went down into the ice room and brought the watermelon back to the galley. He cut it into nine slices and walked around the deck, serving a slice to each man. "This was supposed to be for the trip home," he said, "but now it's a good makeshift breakfast."

It had become harder to hear conversation on the deck, as the wind strengthened. "This might end up being the trip home," Joseph said loudly to the cook as he took a slice.

Doc saved the final piece for Tone, down in the engine room.

The rain had not yet started, but Joseph thought it might come soon. He kept his weather eye open, and his crew secured all the hatches to be ready for the rain. For about an hour they drove straight toward the oncoming winds, heading further offshore. The wind intensified, and the ship rode the waves, tilting slightly starboard, then gently back toward the port side as they rode down the back of each oncoming wave. They did this over and over again in a series of tacking maneuvers. This "broad on the bow" angle of attack, advancing obliquely rather than heading directly into the waves, prevented the full force of the wind and waves from hitting the *Dorcas*.

At last Joseph told Sebastian that it was time for everyone to put on their foul-weather gear. It was important to do this before the flood gates opened.

"You're about to learn why a sou'wester is called a sou'wester!" Merico warned Silva as they made their way down to the forecastle to get into their oilskins, boots, and sou'wester hats.

It was now eight in the morning, and the gale continued to blow as the rain started. The crew above followed Sebastian's orders and made adjustments to the riggings as needed to keep the ship's stability. The *Dorcas* was in almost perfect balance between the forces applied to the keel below and the forces pushing the riding sail above. Sails are useless without the keel, and the keel in turn is useless without a forward thrust; the motor was taking care of that. Both the engineer and the cook were attending to the motor, making sure it was running smoothly and manning the pumps to keep the engine-room dry.

The crew of the *Dorcas* continued with their sail plan for two more arduous hours, riding dauntlessly up and down the waves as the rain blew more heavily and the wind gusted more fiercely. The storm had turned into a squall. Joseph hoped it would become no worse.

* * *

Mary watched the same red sunrise that Joseph had seen out in Georges Bank. She knew it meant a storm was coming. She was concerned for him and for the rest of the crew of the *Dorcas*, though she had absolute confidence in his abilities. He had weathered many storms in his fishing career, and he had always returned home. The worst that had ever happened was the very rare occurrence of a broken trip.

There were a number of household tasks she needed to complete to prepare for the approaching storm. First she went through the house and shut all the windows securely. She could feel the wind gaining strength as it blew through the house. The colder air was starting to cool the overall temperature of the house. Then she turned her attention to the yard. She picked up all the items strewn over the grass, most of them Winnie's toys, and stored them in their proper locations in closets and chests. She also checked the laundry that was hanging on the line. It was still not quite dry; she would check it again later and bring it in before the rain started. She performed all the cleanup tasks quickly, as though she had twelve hands.

At last she began to cook breakfast. Normally she would have enlisted the help of one of her daughters, but this time Mary decided she should send them out of the house to play while they could. She would cook breakfast on her own, alone with her thoughts.

"Winnie," she called, "if you're going to go outside and play today, you'd better do it now. It's going to rain later."

"Good idea, Mama," Winnie replied. She ran down the steps into the yard.

"You too, Kiddo," Mary said, and Kiddo obliged. Her bright red hair, glowing in the sun, matched the auburn and ginger of the sky.

Mary headed into the kitchen. She had already planned on making pancakes; in the event that they lost power later, they would all be glad they had eaten a hardy breakfast. She sifted two cups of flour and added baking powder, sugar, salt, and cream of tartar. Then she separated the whites and yolks from four eggs and beat the whites, stirred in the milk and vanilla, and folded them into the dry ingredients to make the batter.

*Eight more days,* she thought to herself as she cooked the pancakes in the frying pan.

\* \* \*

The *Alice and Wilson* was six miles southeast of the lightship *Nantucket* when Captain Hall made the decision to head out further offshore. They pulled in all of their sails except for the riding sail, and then Captain Hall went down to the engine room.

"Perkins, we're heading out to deeper water. You know what to do."

"You bet, skipper," Perkins replied. "I'll have everything bung up and bilge free, you can count on it."

The *Alice and Wilson* motored northeast through the driving rain and crashing waves, trying to outflank the approaching storm. The ship's ice room was full of thirty swordfish, which provided extra ballast.

\* \* \*

Not far away, the crew on another sworder were also setting up their sail plan. The *Helen E. Murley* was a 40-foot schooner from New Bedford. Captain Kinney explained the situation to his crew of five men: Patrick Baker, Wilson Bushing, William Welch, Francis Maney, and Arthur Reutenhizer. "Our best chance is to head out to sea," he said.

"Aye, captain," Baker said. The rest of the men nodded in

agreement.

"Take down the foresail," the captain commanded, and Welch echoed the order. "Take down the mainsail."

The *Helen E. Murley* drove straight into the gale, heading northeast with only her riding sail.

* * *

Aboard the *Wanderer*, Captain Edwards had decided that the most prudent course of action would be to anchor by the rocks out at Cuttyhunk and wait out what he presumed would be an average summer gale; then, when the winds were more favorable, they would head out to sea on their whaling voyage. A large and heavy ship such as this one, anchored properly, should be secure enough to handle the winds.

What Edwards didn't count on was his anchor chain breaking. Once that happened, the *Wanderer* rocked to and fro and eventually crashed into the rocks at Middle Ground Shoals. At that point the captain wisely ordered the crew to abandon ship.

"Gomes and Freitas," he bellowed, "launch that dory with five men! The rest of you launch in this one with me and Conceiçao!"

"Aye, skipper," the first and second mate cried.

A few hours later, the dory that Gomes and Freitas had launched was saved by the Cuttyhunk Life Saving Station. The other dory, with the skipper aboard, was nowhere to be seen.

* * *

To the northwest, south of Mashpee, the steamship *Augusta* was making an intercoastal shipping run from Boston to New York and got caught up in the storm. The heavy rains and northeast winds caused her to beach at Eastville on Martha's Vineyard. Despite their best efforts, her crew were unable to free themselves, so there they remained, stranded on the beach. The crew found refuge onboard from the gale, safe for the time being.

\* \* \*

Further offshore, Captain Larsen talked with his uncle Charles on the *Anita and Bernice L.* They were a few miles south of the Great South Channel at Georges Bank. "What do you think?" the skipper inquired.

"I don't like the look of it," Charles Larsen said. "We're too far from land to try and outrun it back to shore."

"I agree. Go below and make sure Mr. Mann has that engine running in tip-top shape. We'll need it to operate like clockwork if we're going to head into the belly of the beast."

\* \* \*

Much further north, sixty miles east of Halifax, Captain John Carrancho, the skipper of the *Herbert Parker,* made the opposite decision. He had taken over as skipper of the *Herbert Parker* after Smokey Joe, her former captain, had retired the year before. They were returning from a productive trip to the Sable Island fishing grounds, a trip that would have made Captain Carrancho a highliner for the season had the storm not intervened. He decided to make a beeline toward Maine, with his hold filled with 180,000 pounds of salted fish, in an attempt to outrun the gale back to dry land.

\* \* \*

On the ocean liner *Arabic*, Captain Hickson decided to turn about and face the gale, which proved to be a wise decision, though it resulted in seasickness for many of the passengers. The Mackie and Dickens families had decided to meet in the lounge, to wait out the storm while wearing life vests. They figured that the middle of the ship would be affected least by the rocking motions of the storm. Even so, their children all became violently seasick, regurgitating marmalade, bananas, corn muffins, hot cocoa, and eggs. Their parents collected garbage pails to give them a modicum of dignity and tried to comfort their children as best they could. Soon the ocean water, pouring in, cleared away much of the mess overboard. In fact the water was flowing in and filling the lower level of the *Arabic* at an alarming rate.

* * *

It was now ten o'clock, and the storm was blowing into a veritable hurricane. Joseph manned the helm of the *Dorcas*, clutching the A. P. Stoddart wheel while Sebastian split his time above and below, relaying information.

The skipper had never felt so wet in his entire life. Sebastian came above to give him another update on how things were going in the engine room, then went back to communicate Joseph's latest orders to everyone below. He had to shout over the din of the hurricane. As Joseph looked ahead from the helm, the only two colors he could discern were gray and yellow, a slurry of storm and oilskin. He took another reading from the barometer, straining his eyes in order to read it.

The *Dorcas* continued to drive into the approaching waves. Joseph masterfully steered broad on the starboard bow, then broad on the port bow, returning to the same position before each oncoming wave. They did this again and again for two more hours.

\* \* \*

The *Arabic* had just steamed past the Nantucket Shoals. Captain Hickson stood on the bridge. He could no longer tell which way the winds were blowing; at one point he thought they might be coming from all directions at once.

Then he looked up at an immense shadow above him. It was a giant rogue wave, a hundred feet tall, and it crashed over the side of the *Arabic*. This type of wave is called a comber because of the way it curls over itself as it breaks, collapsing under its own weight as it reveals its white crest.

Captain Hickson could see the crest of the wave rising sixty-five feet above the trough just before it combed over the crow's nest, thirty-five feet above the skipper. The giant wave hove the *Arabic* down to her beam ends for almost a full minute. One more push from the force of the hurricane, and the *Arabic* would have foundered, and all would have been lost.

\* \* \*

At the same moment, a gargantuan wave crashed over the bow of the *Anita and Bernice L.* The small swordfishing schooner capsized and began to fill with water. Captain Larson was washed overboard, along with his uncle Charles and Peter Nelson. When the schooner broke apart, the other five men were trapped below. Selig,

Targett, and Proctor were in the forecastle, while Hilary Conrad and Fritz Mann were in the engine room. They heard the schooner snap in two, and that was the last thing they heard. All eight men sank into the depths of their watery graves.

* * *

Joseph's uneasy feeling grew as the *Dorcas* headed into the fury of the storm. Instinctively he looked over his left shoulder, to get a glance of what might be following him, but having seen nothing in the darkness, he decided not to turn again. His attention had to be focused entirely on what lay ahead. His own fear made him think about the cover of the *Weird Tales* magazine he had seen in the forecastle, the one with the cowboy being chased by a spectral rider.

He glanced at his compass, bracing himself, and recited a stanza from a Coleridge poem: "Like one, that on a lonesome road doth walk in fear and dread. And having once turned round, walks on, and turns no more his head, because he knows a frightful fiend doth close behind him tread." Joseph could barely hear himself speak over the gale-force winds. None of the crew could have heard him either.

During one of his tacks, Joseph saw an enormous white-crested rogue wave looming over the port rail. He clutched the wheel as hard as he could. When the wave crashed, the *Dorcas* was hove down onto her beam ends.

"Death by water!" Joseph exclaimed. He heard a loud clang of breaking metal, and he knew what was likely to come next, so he breathed in deeply and filled his lungs with oxygen. The gear on the wheel had snapped, and the centrifugal force, spinning in the opposite direction, forced the wheel to whip and turn rapidly. That movement, along with the force of the wave, launched Joseph over the starboard rail into the cruel foamy sea.

Joseph fought like a demon to get to the surface. He realized that his legs were tangled up by rigging underwater, so he reached for the knife sheathed below his shoulder. He had to cut through four strands of rope to free himself. It was fortunate that he had been able to inhale before being washed overboard because it took him almost twenty seconds to regain the surface. Once there he inhaled deeply and started to breathe again.

Above him was the silhouette of the almost capsized *Dorcas*. Then he was washed underwater again in the swell. Still alive and still snorting oxygen, he fought to stay at the surface, struggling against the added drag of his oilskins. The *Dorcas* had flipped over onto her starboard rail, and there was an alarming amount of flotsam in the water.

He could feel his rosary beads pressed against his wet neck. If he could swim toward the debris, he might be able to grab hold of a spar and maybe, just maybe, crawl back onboard. Then he inhaled some seawater and started to cough. The shock of his mental and physical distress had started to overtake him. He coughed again and was pulled underwater once more.

\* \* \*

Captain Brown made the decision to head out to deep water. His schooner, the *Christie A. Cox,* took a hit from one of the large waves, but fortunately the damage was not as severe as it was for other ships in the fleet. The *Christie A. Cox* lost most of her forerigging, and the foremast became a bit wobbly and needed to be secured by the crew, but they were still above the surface. They did what they could and powered on into the tempest, determined to make it back to shore.

* * *

The *Helen E. Murley* was still following the sail plan that had been set by Captain Kinney. An enormous wave washed over the schooner from New Bedford, and as it rose Patrick Baker yelled, "Skipper!" Captain Kinney looked up. It was the last thing he ever saw before his mind was consumed by the darkness. *Mother of God!* the skipper thought.

The wave broke the small schooner in half. Bushing, Welch, Maney, and Reutenhizer, down below, saw nothing but heard it all. The room they were in flooded with water, and all six men were lost in the pressure vacuum that caused the middle of the ship to implode into the abyss. What was left of the *Helen E. Murley* foundered quickly.

* * *

Sebastian knew he must hold on tightly to the handrail in the stairwell. Up turned to the left, and down rolled to the right. All his knowledge of life and direction was tossed overboard in a forward roll. Everything went sideways, and the world was oriented wrong. Yet even with the disorientation, he could see through the portal onto the top deck. Right before the moment when the comber wave crashed over the port side, he had seen the yellow-rubber silhouettes of Domingoes working topside with Merico and Brown.

When the massive wave broke over the ship, Sebastian heard a loud snap as the main mast splintered, and the *Dorcas* listed onto her starboard side. The falling mast swept Domingoes, Brown, and Merico over the starboard rail into the water, while the bow rose up and the stern fell. Then Sebastian heard other deafening creaks and snaps—the sounds of large pieces of wood breaking. The *Dorcas* hove down onto her beam ends. Both spars were under water.

Sebastian didn't have time to check on the men in the engine room as he had planned. He could only hope that everyone below had been holding onto something when the wave crashed, and that they had been able to man the pumps, keep the engine room dry, and ensure that the motor was still running. Sebastian himself had to turn his attention topside. Keeping his balance with difficulty, he climbed onto the port rail, the only part of the *Dorcas* where he could find solid footing.

"Joseph!" Sebastian yelled, when he saw that his brother was no longer at the helm. "Joseph!" he yelled again, even louder. The din of the winds was now joined by the roar of the ship's propeller, racing through the air instead of underwater where it should have been.

The other three men were nowhere to be seen, washed overboard along with his brother. The *Dorcas* had flipped almost all the way over onto her starboard side. All four of the dories had lurched forward into the sea, breaking free of their cleats and the ropes that had tied them down. The anchor had vanished. Both masts had flipped over, their tops underwater. All the booms and gaffs had broken off and were dangling over the starboard rail, which itself was underwater and taking a beating as the spars battered the rail and her stanchions.

From Sebastian's vantage point, the outlook appeared dire for his brother and his crew-mates. He could see no future for the *Dorcas*.

* * *

The *Alice and Wilson* drove straight into the swirling chaos, five nautical miles from the Nantucket Shoals. A large wave crashed over her port rail, freeing a nest of dories and sweeping Captain Hall overboard. He fought desperately to find a hold among the flotsam. Then, when the wave washed back in the opposite direction, it carried the captain back to the schooner.

"John!" his brother yelled. The captain heard the voice and turned toward it.

On board, his brother saw him in the foam and threw him a line. The skipper climbed aboard, fortunate to escape with only a few bruised ribs. "Thanks, brother!" the captain said.

They continued to fight the storm, maintaining their plan to head further offshore. Captain Hall regained control of the helm despite the swelling pain in his ribcage. Then he heard the snap of wood and saw the main mast break off at the base. It carried Marques and King overboard with it, but they were able to claw their way onto the mast, which floated near the *Alice and Wilson*. The crew threw them a rope.

"Ho! Grab the line, I'll pull you back!" Malloy yelled. Silva helped Malloy pull them back onto the schooner, and the two men both climbed aboard.

The crew fought for their lives as the pig-iron ballast flew up like projectiles through the floor boards, adding another dangerous hazard to their already deadly situation.

Once more a giant wave hove the schooner down. This time the foremast broke off.

"Watch out!" Marques yelled as the mast flew at him and the other crew-members topside.

The big mast cleared the deck of spars, rigging, and gear, as well as the three men. James Holland, Joaquim Dores, and Manuel Marques were carried overboard. They had been knocked unconscious and sank quickly. They were never heard from again.

* * *

Fortunately, the center of mass of the *Arabic* had allowed her to regain her righting arm, and she slowly returned to an upright position. However, the chaotic wave had caused much damage to her structure and many injuries to her passengers.

Inside the lounge, at the midpoint of the ocean liner, the Dickens and Mackie families could hear the smashing of bulkheads and the crashing of furniture. They watched out the windows as lifeboats washed overboard. Desperately they huddled together as the windows broke and water poured into the interior rooms of the *Arabic*. A column of water flowed into the lounge, and a large piece of furniture raced toward the Mackie family and buffeted them against the inner wall. A bookcase surged toward them. The force of the flow trapped the whole family behind the bookcase, barely above water, captured in the swell.

Frederick Dickens and his oldest son were swept out of the lounge by the deluge of water—knocked down to the floor and carried out the doorway. They were about to be washed overboard when Frederick grabbed onto the railing of one of the few lifeboats that had not yet been washed overboard. He clutched his son's wrist with his other hand, pulled the child up beside him, and then held on for dear life. T. H. Owens, one of the deck stewards of the *Arabic* was washed overboard nearby, but then was fortunately tossed onboard again in the wave's backwash. When he regained his footing on the deck, he pulled Frederick and his son over the railing and led them back to safety in the interior of the ocean liner, where they reunited with their family.

Had Captain Hickson been in front of a mirror, he would have seen his face turn pale. He had just received the somber report that the engine room had begun to flood. And to make matters worse, the engineers had reported that many barrels had smashed open and oil was now mixing in with the seawater, creating a very dangerous situation. The skipper needed to get the *Arabic* to safe harbor as fast as possible, or else all the souls on board might be lost.

\* \* \*

Sebastian knew that his brother, Brown, Merico, and Domingoes had been washed overboard. Hearing shouts, he searched for signs of life in the water over the starboard rail. He saw some of his crew-members, identifiable only by the obscured silhouettes of their sou'westers and oilskins at the surface of the water. They had grabbed onto the gaffs and spars that had washed overboard but were still attached to the *Dorcas* by the rigging.

Sebastian and Silva helped each other crawl precariously onto the port rail. They threw lifesaving lines over the starboard side of the *Dorcas*, and the three men in the water were able to swim toward the ropes. First Domingoes climbed back aboard, with the help of Sebastian. Next came Brown, who was hurt badly, with a bloody face and a twisted leg. Silva met him at the edge of the rail. "We've got you, dory mate," he said as he helped Brown climb aboard. The last to climb up was Merico.

"Joseph!" Sebastian hollered one more time. "JOSEPH!" He knew what his next move must be. If his brother was anywhere near the *Dorcas*, he would have found a way to hold onto the flotsam of the spars and rigging and would now be hanging desperately onto the *Dorcas,* in the way that a drowning man will cling to anyone and anything. But he could see no sign of Joseph, and he couldn't put the rest of the crew in peril by looking any further. So he gave the next command: "Axes now! Knives!"

All of them who could move scavenged for anything sharp they could find. Fortunately Joseph had suggested to Doc that he put the sharp instruments where they could be easily retrieved in an emergency. The men climbed down into the galley, fetched the knives and axes, and struggled back up again to the deck. Under

Sebastian's command, they chopped off the main mast and the foremast at their stems. Two men lay down on their stomachs over the port rail, holding a third man by his legs so that he could chop at the mast stems.

Sebastian could barely hear the thunks of the axe over the noise from the hurricane. Both men finished at the same time, and the *Dorcas*, which had been flipped over sideways, now turned back over into an almost normal position, free from the drag of the two masts that had hove her down. The crew had to hold on for dear life as the *Dorcas* righted herself.

It took a few seconds for the crew to reorient themselves and regain their balance and footing. Once they did, Sebastian instructed them to cut off any remaining rigging and spars, so as to streamline what was left of the schooner. He noticed that the bowsprit had splintered and was now dangling off the bow. Domingoes grabbed it and chopped it off with an axe. The striker salvaged his horseshoe, tucked it into his belt, and tossed the remainder of the bowsprit overboard to join the rest of the flotsam.

As Sebastian gave his instructions, he took advantage of their new sound footing and went to check on the wheel. As soon as he grabbed it, he realized that it was turning with no resistance, which meant the steering system was broken—mostly likely the gear where the worm screw was connected to the rudder pole—and had thus become completely useless.

He looked toward the starboard side. Most of the rail had been battered away. He decided to focus his attention below, for now that the *Dorcas* had righted herself he could no longer hear the hum of the propeller, and everything would depend on whether or not the motor had stopped.

He feared the worst, and his instincts were correct. The sudden turn of the *Dorcas* had flooded the engine room and the forecastle. Quickly Sebastian thought out a new strategy. He helped the wounded Brown below. Given his injuries, he wouldn't be able to help much topside, so Sebastian figured he could be of use with fuel or the pumps.

When they reached the engine room, he found Silva, Doc, and Tone desperately manning the pumps to get the water line below the motor.

"Tone, we must get that motor running," Sebastian said. It was loud in the engine room, but not nearly as chaotic as it was topside. All eight of the men were now down below, either in the forecastle or aft in the engine room, where they manned the pumps while being tossed around violently in the tempest.

Eventually they pumped the water level down below the engine. As Tone reached down to try to start it up again, they all gathered around to ask the Queen of Heaven to help them get back home alive. Sebastian had something special to say: "If we make it out of this, we'll all feed the poor and get the Crown of the Holy Ghost, just like the crew of the *Mary P. Mesquita.*"

"We'll all be crowned Imperators," Doc assured them.

They held hands, and Sebastian led them in an old fisherman's prayer. Then Tone pulled the cord, and the motor started. If they ever made it back to Gloucester, they would have to fulfill their promise by donating their pay from the trip to fund a *Sopas do Espirito Santo*, the Holy Ghost soup.

"And as a tribute to Joseph," Sebastian added, "we'll all go to the crowning ceremony wearing our oilskins, sou'westers, and rubber boots, just like Smokey Joe." The entire crew agreed wholeheartedly.

Now, with engine power but without the ability to steer, they were about to face the biggest test of their nautical skills they had ever encountered, as they endured the hurricane.

It was critical that they find an alternate steering method. Sebastian looked at the crew and saw that Domingoes appeared to have had an epiphany. The solution, explained the striker, was to turn the rudder pole manually. "We need to hack into the wheel box," he said.

Grabbing a hatchet, he went topside and started chopping at the wood siding of the wheel box. Much of it had already been battered away by the storm. Sebastian grabbed another ax and assisted. Soon they gained access to the rudder pole inside, and Sebastian saw that the gear connected to the wheel had snapped, just as he had suspected.

Domingoes came up with the idea of lashing harpoons across the rudder pole so that they could use them as a makeshift lever to turn the pole. First they lashed two of the harpoons to the pole with some manilla rope. But when they tried to turn the harpoons, they creaked and groaned uselessly against the rudder pole: there was too much give, and they couldn't gain enough leverage to turn the rudder. Then Domingoes had another idea. They untied the harpoons, and he took out his horseshoe and forced it down onto the gear on the rudder pole, creating a fulcrum. Tone, catching onto the train of this logic, brought out two large wrenches which he attached securely to each side of the horseshoe.

Then once again they lashed the harpoons to the pole with manilla rope. This time the system worked. It took two men to operate their new steering method, but they had regained control of the ship. When Sebastian and Domingoes turned the harpoons to the left, the rudder turned to the right. When they turned the harpoons to the right, the rudder turned to the left. The *Dorcas* could now be steered.

Tone and Brown stayed below to ensure that the motor continued to run, while the rest of the crew manned the pumps. Miraculously, the *Dorcas* had continued to face forward into the storm, and now they could guide her again.

With the loss of Joseph, Sebastian, the first mate, had become the helmsman. They had a workable rudder and a motorized propeller pushing them forward. There was no longer any drag from the masts, sails, or rigging. The keel was doing an effective job of keeping them upright and moving them in a relatively straight line. And the new, lower profile of the *Dorcas* allowed her to stay afloat and power straight through the hurricane.

\* \* \*

The *Christie A. Cox* was in a dire situation. The damage had started to mount, and although the small schooner managed to hold together through the worst of the gale, the waves were still large and the winds still howled. One of her fuel tanks had washed overboard, and it was unlikely that their remaining fuel would last through the night. Captain Brown had heroically lashed himself to the helm and drove the schooner for ten more hours—an eternity to the stalwart skipper.

* * *

The *Alice and Wilson* was in grave danger of sinking. She had no engine power, and her rudder had snapped off. The little schooner was taking on water at an alarming rate, and the pump handle had broken off and was nowhere to be found. The crew bailed for their lives with buckets. For eight hours the five men took turns with two draw buckets. Each man bailed with fervor, then passed the buckets to a fresher man when his arms gave out from exhaustion, while the small schooner was tossed around by the gale.

"I'm almost spent," Antoine Silva said, as Fonce Malloy relieved him and started to bail.

"Me too," James Hall said, as his brother, the captain, relieved him. Perkins was at the ready and would relieve the next man to tire. He saw something floating by his feet in the ankle-deep water: a four-foot section of a bowsprit. With a sudden grin, he picked it up and showed it to the rest of the crew.

They knew exactly what he was thinking. "Pump away, Mr. Perkins!" the skipper ordered. All the men helped to remove what was left of the pump's broken handle, and then they replaced it with the spar, which was an almost perfect fit.

"Our luck has changed," Perkins said to his crewmates as he manned the pump. He worked as though his life depended upon it— which it did. Each of the men felt a newfound vigor and wellspring of strength.

For the next eight hours they manned the pump, somehow finding the energy to keep up with the steady flow of water that rushed into the schooner. Gradually they gained ground and started to overtake the leak. They had no concept of time. They were thirsty and starving.

* * *

In the wake of the storm, at 6:30 p.m., a rainbow appeared over Portuguese Hill in Gloucester. The city had received nearly six inches of rain from the storm. There were trees down all over town, including the three majestic willow trees by the Hotel Thorwald.

The Coast Guard and the Harbormaster both had a very busy evening with all the cleanup. But, overall, there was minimal property damage for such an aggressive storm. Most of its fury had been unleashed offshore. The city of Gloucester got busy after the storm, cutting away the fallen trees, turning the power back on and clearing away the detritus. The people of Gloucester tended to the jetsam while the Harbormaster and the Coast Guard tended to the flotsam.

Out on Edward Lufkin's farm, one of the farm boys went out to the barn to tend to the cattle as soon as the storm subsided. He was surprised to find a newly born heifer. He watched the sunset to the west with Gloucester's newest resident. He convinced Mr.

Lufkin to name the newly born calf, "Storm".

\* \* \*

"We've been without power all day," Birdie said to her mother. "The last thing you should have to do now is cook a big dinner. Why don't we order some take out? I can take Kiddo out to get it. It's time we teach her a little responsibility with money."

Her coaxing worked. The phones were now back up and running across the whole city. Birdie listened in the kitchen as Mama dialed 1970 on their rotary phone and placed their order of chop suey and chow mein from the Royal Restaurant.

Mama then gave some money to Kiddo. "This should be enough," she said as she handed Kiddo a few bills. "There and back, no dilly-dallying."

"Okay, Mama," Kiddo replied.

She and Birdie hurried out the front door and down the hill. As they walked, they watched the soft diffuse glow of red in the sky as the sun descended toward the horizon in the west. Birdie smiled when she saw Kiddo's red hair glowing in the light.

"Red sky at night, sailor's delight," Kiddo said. "That's what Pa always says."

They passed by a group of big-city artists from New York who had been inspired by the colors in the sky. It had become fashionable for artists to spend the summer in Gloucester, using the town and the harbor as backdrops for their work. The two sisters watched as the artists jockeyed for position to get the best view of the harbor at sunset.

163

It took them about five more minutes to reach the small restaurant on Main Street. Along the way they saw lots of unripe apples and beach plums, left behind in the storm drains—evidence of the hurricane. The winds had been strong enough to blow them off the trees.

Their food was ready when they got there, tucked into a couple of brown paper bags. Kiddo paid the bill and collected their change under Birdie's watchful eye. Then they walked out of the small restaurant and began to retrace their steps.

Captain Blackburn passed them on the sidewalk, and Birdie was acutely aware that her little sister was staring at the stumps of his hands as he walked past them.

"Good evening, Birdie," Captain Blackburn said.

"Good evening, Captain," she replied.

"What happened to his hands?" Kiddo asked when they were out of earshot.

"He was in a tragic fishing accident. Pa has told me that story a few times. He was with another fisherman in a dory during a winter storm, and they got lost. The other man was getting sick, so Captain Blackburn lashed his own hands to the oars to row the sick man back to shore. But the other man died, and Captain Blackburn lost all his fingers to frostbite because he lost his mittens. The other man was frozen solid by the time he got the dory back to dry land."

Both girls shuddered, and Kiddo said nothing for the rest of the walk back home.

On the way up the hill they passed Burnham's Field, which

had been completely flooded during the storm.

When they got home, they all sat at the table and Mama led them in saying grace. Then she passed around the food containers, and everyone helped themselves with a serving spoon or fork.

"I hope Pa and Uncle Sebastian are okay. I hope the storm didn't hit them," Birdie said.

"Don't you worry," Mama said to her daughters. "Pa knows how to handle a storm. He's one of the most experienced captains in the fleet."

They ate their dinner in silence, then all helped to clear the table. They worked together to do the dishes.

Le tried to find something to listen to on the radio, but all the stations were obscured by static. "This is impossible," she said. Giving up, she decided to find something to read instead. Then Birdie tried her hand at the radio, and within a few seconds she found a station broadcasting loud and clear. It was playing a new jazz song she had heard before.

Later that night, after her younger sisters had all gone to bed, Birdie went out for the night to the Long Beach Pavilion, where she met up with Julia Silva, Joseph Silva's wife, for the Elks and Friends dance. They were close in age and were close friends too, because of the family connection.

"Get ready," Birdie said to Julia. "I'm going to win one of those prizes when they release the balloons."

"How fun! What a nice change of pace from all those cake walks," Julia replied.

Hundreds of balloons of many different colors—red, white, blue, green—were released from nets just below the ceiling to fall onto the dance floor. Inside five of the balloons were winning tickets that entitled each winner to a box of fine chocolates.

The dance floor became a cacophony of popping balloons as the frenzied dancers stomped and stomped in search of the winning tickets. Julia stomped. Birdie stomped. Her white balloon burst and revealed a silver ticket inside. "I won, I won!" Birdie cried. Julia congratulated her on her good fortune. They held hands and jumped up and down.

\* \* \*

*What a terrible way to become a skipper for the first time,* Sebastian thought as he stood at the helm. Domingoes was with him, guiding the makeshift rudder. Sebastian would occasionally give a course correction, and the two of them would steer accordingly.

Sebastian manned the helm of the *Dorcas*. It was brighter than the night before. The storm had lost a lot of its strength. The wind had died down, and the moon was reflected on the breaking surf. Sebastian could see the waves as he steered through them at full throttle. He could smell the smoke from the engine mixing with the salt in the air. He could hear the waves as they broke. Every once in a while a splash of salt water would find its way onto his face.

He thought about his brother. He still felt there might have been something he could have done differently. He thought about his own wife and daughters and wondered what they were thinking and feeling. He felt guilty, belatedly, that he had not given more thought to them since the hurricane hit. He knew they must be worried about him, and this made him even more resolved to bring the *Dorcas* home.

"You realize what this means, right?" Domingoes asked him. "You're the skipper now."

"Yes, I know. And that makes you my first mate."

"I don't know if I'm ready for that," Domingoes said.

"I hear you," Sebastian said. *And I guess that makes me the last of the Silveiras,* he thought as he drove the *Dorcas* through the night.

# Bright Moonlight

Phlebas the Phoenician, a fortnight dead,
Forgot the cry of gulls, and the deep sea swell
And the profit and loss.

A current under sea
Picked his bones in whispers. As he rose and fell
He passed the stages of his age and youth
Entering the whirlpool.

Gentile or Jew
O you who turn the wheel and look to windward,
Consider Phlebas,
Who was once handsome and tall as you.

"Death by Water," *The Waste Land,* T.S. Eliot

***Wednesday, August 27, 1924.***

It was now past midnight, and the gale had moved further offshore, northeast past Nova Scotia. But east of Georges Bank, the crew of the *Dorcas* was still at the mercy of the stormy sea for hours. At last Sebastian sensed that the tempest had begun to subside. Early in the morning, well after midnight, it broke.

Sebastian wondered if there was a word or phrase for the feeling he was experiencing—that feeling of guilt when you have survived something but someone you loved did not. The Portuguese seemed to have several unique words for complex emotions, but he could not think of anything in any language that gave a name to how he felt. He realized it was not helpful to keep asking himself, *Why not me? Did I do something wrong? Was there something different I could have done?*

169

But still he continued to think that it should have been him instead of his brother. He couldn't help but follow that train of thought.

At the makeshift helm, next to what was left of the wheel box, Sebastian and Domingoes drove the *Dorcas* toward land. They had fuel, food, and water. The worst of the hurricane was over. And now Sebastian finally realized that he had lost his brother forever. He was gone.

Sebastian's emotions overwhelmed him for a brief spell. Then he attempted to regain himself. Although he still could not really accept the events of the past day, he had seven crew-members to think about, and although the immediate danger of the storm had passed, the *Dorcas* was a battered hulk with no sails and only a makeshift steering method. Fortunately, they had plenty of fuel and the motor was still running.

The seas were still very rough, and the *Dorcas* was 150 miles offshore. The crew took turns trying to catch up on sleep. Sebastian decided he must get a little rest too, so he went down to the captain's cabin to lie down on one of the bunks. Merico and Murray took over at the helm so that Domingoes could also try to sleep.

Sebastian dreamed the way desperate people who have been deprived of sleep often dream, drifting deep into their subconscious minds. He was now the skipper of his own schooner, the *Joseph Silveira*. It was the first of many trips, and the schooner was fitting out. Including himself, he had a crew of nine. Some of them would have to do double duty on the way out. The forecastle table still needed to be constructed, as did some of the lockers and cabinets.

They anchored for the night by Sankaty Head. Sebastian was at the bow at sunset. At the last burst of twilight, he saw something emerge from the water. It grabbed at the anchor chain as it surfaced—a large orange tentacle from below the depths. He woke up, his heart racing.

Not wanting to revisit the nightmare, Sebastian decided to return topside and let some of the other crew get some rest. He took his position again at the helm. Over the next hour, the clouds abated and bright moonlight illuminated everything left on the deck of the *Dorcas*. The welcome light allowed the crew-members who were on duty to find one of the lanterns, and once it was lit Sebastian located one of the foghorns and sounded a long, slow blast. They also found some more food in the galley, and they still had plenty of drinking water. Sebastian ate some hard-tack crackers and drank some water.

The moon wasn't yet close to full; it was still in the third quarter, waning toward the crescent. The many scattered clouds trailing in the wake of the storm created a dreamlike atmosphere in the moonlight.

Sebastian continued to blow the foghorn every two minutes for almost two hours, pushing the handle down slowly to create as long a blast as possible. Then, to the joy of the crew, they finally heard a horn in the distance bellowing in reply, no more than a mile or two away. They had made contact with another vessel, and after he had blown the horn a few more times and listened intently for each reply, it became clear to Sebastian that the other ship must be drawing closer to them: the other horn was gradually getting louder.

A half-hour later, they reunited with—and were eventually

rescued by—the schooner *Funchal*. Their prayer for succor had been answered.

\* \* \*

Captain Carrancho had guided his crew through the storm successfully. The *Herbert Parker* still had a long way to go to get to dry land in Maine, but her motor was still running, and their hold was still full of 180,000 pounds of salted fish. She maintained her course as the sun rose in the wake of the storm. The skipper thought only of his wife.

\* \* \*

By six o'clock in the morning, the gale had diminished tremendously. It made landfall once more at Prince Edward Island, continuing its northeasterly turn, but by this time it had weakened down to a Category One hurricane, with sustained wind gusts of only 90 miles per hour.

\* \* \*

Birdie watched as Mama prepared breakfast in the kitchen, taking out dishes and silverware, eggs, *linguiça*, and *bolos* for toast. She prepared to cook the eggs.

"I'm sure they'll be fine," Birdie assured her sisters as they helped Mama prepare breakfast.

"Yes, Pa always knows what to do out on the water. He's quite stalwart as a skipper," Mama agreed. She poached the eggs while Kiddo and Winnie set the table for breakfast.

"Fork and knife on this side, spoon on the other," Kiddo instructed Winnie. "And don't forget to set a place for Pa."

Once the food was ready, Birdie and Le helped Mama bring it out to the table. It was a silent breakfast, for they were all in somber, worried moods. They prayed for their husband, father, uncle, and cousin, and for the rest of the crew. It had now been seven days since the *Dorcas* had sailed out, and as of yet they had received no news of the crew's fate.

At last Birdie broke the silence. "You know, it was almost exactly a year ago that Pa marched in that parade with the Bugle and Drum Corps for the Fraternity Club." Last summer Joseph had played in the 35-member marching band as one of the 34 buglers, along with one lone cymbal player, as part of Gloucester's tercentenary parade.

"He looked so handsome in that uniform—white cap, blue shirt, white duck trousers and leggings," Mama recalled.

"And he played the bugle so well," Birdie said.

"They won an award for their performance," Kiddo said proudly.

"See, you're not the only one in the family with musical talent," Le said to Birdie; she could never resist an opportunity to bicker with her older sister.

Birdie could have taken the bait and bickered back, but instead she decided to extend an olive branch. She went upstairs to her bedroom and then rejoined her sister in the kitchen. "Have a chocolate, Le," she said, handing over the box she had won at the dance the night before.

"Thanks, Birdie!" Le exclaimed. Then she admitted, "I

suppose I will miss you when you head away to college."

"I'll miss you too, Le."

Birdie was very worried about Pa. She watched as Mama silently cleared the table and began to wash the pots and pans, the dishes, and the silverware.

* * *

The *Alice and Wilson* was a helpless hulk. She drifted at the mercy of the sea all morning. A steamer passed by in the distance but did not hear her horn. A tanker did the same an hour later, with the same result. From where they were, the crew couldn't get to the forecastle to retrieve supplies. They had no food and no water. Their situation was desperate.

Another steamer passed by in the distance, too far away to hear their horn. The crew decided they needed to fashion a visible signal. They lashed an American flag upside down onto a pole, to indicate their distress.

"Keep sounding the horn," Captain Hall said to Perkins. "One of these ships is bound to hear it. And now that we have a distress flag, someone will realize what's happened to us."

* * *

The Coast Guard launched the cutter *Acushnet* from Woods Hole, and shortly thereafter she found the distressed *Augusta* beached in the sand at Eastville. It took some doing and the help of a Coast Guard crew with heavy equipment, but after a spell of hard work they were able to tow the freighter into deeper water, where she could start moving again under her own power.

The *Augusta* continued her trip to New York, while the *Acushnet* continued her search-and-rescue operations. She joined up with the cutter *Ossipee*, which had launched from Portland, and for the next few days the two Coast Guard vessels zigzagged their way across every inch of Georges Bank, in a desperate attempt to search for survivors. The cutter *Tampa* searched further southeast.

\* \* \*

Captain Hickson had heroically guided the *Arabic* back to New York, after turning into the storm and then reversing direction out at the Nantucket Shoals. The seventy-five injured passengers and crew were staged topside as they docked, laid on mattresses strewn across the deck, ready to be evacuated upon landing. Twelve of the most seriously injured passengers were sent to nearby New York hospitals in ambulances.

The victim in the most critical condition was Patrick Karney, one of the ship's firemen, who had been smashed against a beam by the floodwater. He had broken his back while in the line of duty, trying to put out a fire in the engine room. Another two dozen passengers needed urgent medical attention, which was administered on the deck by the many doctors and surgeons who were waiting for them when the *Arabic* docked.

The Dickens and Mackie families both disembarked. They gathered themselves and their belongings, and eventually caught their connecting trains to Wisconsin and California respectively. It was the last time that either family would take an ocean liner to Europe.

Gloucester was now back open for business, and one of the key meetings of the day was a planning session for the Tercentenary Permanent Memorial Association. Even though the primary celebration of the city's three hundredth anniversary had already occurred last summer, the association was still busy with their final order of business: the memorial statue. Smokey Joe was an advisor to the committee, representing the Master Mariners' Association.

During the tercentenary celebration, the city had held a contest to design the memorial statue. The winner was an English sculptor named Leonard Craske. His winning sketch was titled "The Helmsman," and he had based it on countless hours of study down at the harbor and out on the ocean in schooners, where he observed Gloucester fishermen in action. He drew them, photographed them, and went down to the sea with them.

At today's meeting, which included Craske, they hoped to finalize the design of the statue. There was one flaw in the original sketch, according to the Master Mariners' Association: the skipper wasn't wearing foul-weather gear, and this didn't seem appropriate.

Smokey Joe addressed the committee to explain the Association's position. "If the statue is going to be part of a memorial to those who were lost at sea, many of whom were lost in foul weather, then it should show the helmsman wearing oilskins and a sou'wester hat."

"I think that's a mighty fine suggestion," Craske said. "I'll incorporate the change and send a revised sketch before we create the cast at the Gorham foundry. To stay on schedule, I'll head down to Providence to work out the details of the casting tomorrow."

Smokey Joe appreciated Craske's willingness to take a thoughtful suggestion. A compromise had been reached, and the design was finalized for the statue that would come to be known as the Gloucester Fishermen's Memorial. With their business concluded, Carleton H. Parsons, who was the president of the Tercentenary Permanent Memorial Association, adjourned the meeting.

* * *

On the *Funchal*, Sebastian sat quietly and watched as Doc tended to Brown's twisted leg. The crew of the *Funchal* did everything they could to accommodate the crew from the *Dorcas*. The cook brought out water, then some hard tack, and lastly some coffee.

The first mate of the *Funchal* gave them blankets. "Feel free to get out of those wet things and warm up," he said. His crew collected the wet clothes and spread out the shirts and pants around the stove in the galley to dry them off.

The crew of the *Dorcas* wrapped themselves in the blankets while Sebastian listened to Doc's diagnosis of Brown's leg injury. "It doesn't seem to be broken, but you've got some tissue damage—probably a ligament, I would bet. But keep in mind, I'm not really a doctor. I'll try to put it in a splint, so we can keep it immobilized until a real doctor can look at you."

Sebastian gathered some rope and a few poles to make the splint.

While Doc worked on Brown's leg, the crew of the *Dorcas* told their story to the men of the *Funchal*. Sebastian needed sleep; the little he had gotten overnight had not been enough. He listened as Domingoes, Brown, and Merico described how the three of them had been washed overboard but, by the grace of the Lord, had beaten the odds and been pulled back aboard by Sebastian and Silva. Sebastian shook his head. Why hadn't his brother had the same good fortune?

"You take one of the bunks and sleep first," Silva said to Brown, who had started to nod off.

"You sure? It's nice of you to offer."

"Dory mate's code," Silva said.

"Dory mate's code." Brown agreed. He settled into one of the available bunks and drifted off to sleep.

Domingoes added to their story. Sebastian listened to the striker describing what it had been like to get washed overboard—how the impact of the spar had made him exhale heavily, removing the air in his lungs that would have given him some buoyancy. As he fell into the cold salt water, he fought to regain the surface and fill his lungs with air. "I saw something white in the water. I thought of my beloved Rosella, and I imagined it was her. I reached for her. The back swell of the wave pushed me forward, and with my outstretched arms I was able to grab the line attached to the spar dangling overboard. I shouted for help, as loudly as I could."

"Our luck certainly changed after Sebastian got us back on board," Merico added. "When he had us chop off the masts, that righted the ship, and then we could pump and get the engine going."

"Our skipper made the right call, heading into the storm," Domingoes said. "But Sebastian, he is the one who saved us. He knew what to do to right the ship, get the engine room pumped, and get us moving again. Sebastian saved us all."

"Well, you certainly pulled a horseshoe out of your rear end to get us steering again," Merico said. He recounted the tale of Domingoes' horseshoe, the wrenches, and the harpoons.

Then Sebastian listened as Tone told the tale from the engine room's perspective. "As soon as we rolled over, I thought that was it," Tone admitted. "The engine room started filling with water right after we rolled. Doc and I tried pumping, but we were all sideways. And the water was splashing everywhere."

"When Sebastian got us right side up again, that's when I felt some hope," Murray said. "Everyone came down to pump, and once we got the motor above the water line, we all said a prayer, and all the Portuguese guys started talking about becoming emperor for the day and walking up the hill in our fishing gear, just like Smokey Joe."

"We survived because we all worked together," Sebastian said. "And because of that, our prayer was answered."

"Our skipper saw your lights, and we heard your horn," the *Funchal* cook said. "At first we couldn't believe what we were seeing. There were no masts! Then the skipper yelled down to the engineer to coax a little more speed out of her."

Merico yawned. It was contagious and soon spread to the other crew-members. Most of the crew of the *Dorcas* were drifting off. As Sebastian sank into sleep, he heard a distant conversation between two crew-members of the *Funchal*.

"Just like Smokey Joe," one *Funchal* man said to the other.

It would take them twenty more hours to reach Gloucester, on Sebastian's estimation. The interval would give the crews of both schooners time to catch up on sleep and eat some food.

# Back to Gloucester

On reef and bar our schooners drove
Before the wind, before the swell;
By the steep sand cliffs their ribs were stove,—
Long, long their crews the tale shall tell!
Of the Gloucester fleet are wrecks threescore;
Of the Province sail two hundred more
Were stranded in that tempest fell.

*The Lord's-Day Gale*, Edmund Clarence Stedman

***Thursday, August 28, 1924.***

The crew of the *Alice and Wilson* was still in terrible straits. They had had nothing to eat or drink for a day and a half, and now they were at the brink of doom. They continued to blow the horn and fly their distress flag, hopelessly. All through the night they drifted, just barely visible in the scattered moonlight through the clouds. In the morning, the sun rose. They were starving and parched. No help came. The members of the crew were becoming desperate.

\* \* \*

Things were not quite as dire aboard the second (and yet to be accounted for) dory from the *Wanderer*. A life-saving boat from the Cuttyhunk Life Saving Station had heard their distress horn, and their rescue was now imminent.

"Keep blowing that horn," Captain Edwards instructed.

"Aye, skipper," Conceiçao said. The third mate slowly pushed and pulled the handle of the foghorn to create one long blast.

"Now I know why Tom decided to retire from whaling."

Not long after this, the life-saving crew found them. The entire crew of the *Wanderer* had survived the storm. The *Wanderer* herself, however, had not. Earlier that morning, what was left of her hull had broken apart at the Sow and Pigs lightship, and thus concluded the final trip of the last square-rigged whaling bark from the fabled New Bedford fleet.

* * *

Captain Brown and his crew had also lasted through the storm. The *Christie A. Cox* was far offshore when she ran out of fuel, but she still had her masts and sails and her crew. It took expert sailing and navigational skill to survive, but the captain and crew were up to the task. They sailed back toward Gloucester. It was slow going, as they were tacking against the wind, but they got closer and closer to home.

* * *

By dawn, the eye of the storm had moved much further northeast, past Newfoundland. It was now a tropical storm, with sustained wind gusts of only 60 miles per hour. Later that morning it disappeared far offshore and finally dissipated into a random set of winds that were absorbed by the North Atlantic Ocean.

* * *

Sebastian was at the helm of the *Funchal*, standing with Captain Sears and holding a mug of coffee, when the sun rose behind them. At their current rate of speed, he expected that they would make it back to Gloucester by late afternoon. He felt the wind on his face and saw the powder-blue sky at the moment when the sun peeked over the horizon. Almost immediately he felt its warm glow on his cheeks. There were a few clouds out, but none due east to obscure the view.

Sebastian thought about his wife and daughters as he felt the spray on his face. He contemplated his career options. Fortunately he had had some education, which increased the possibilities. Slowly the orange horizon blended into the blue sky of morning.

"Thanks again for everything, Captain Sears," Sebastian said.

"Don't mention it. I'm sorry about your brother. He was a legend and a good friend."

For the rest of the morning and into the afternoon, Sebastian and his crew helped out where they could, while the *Funchal* motored forward with the *Dorcas* still under tow.

Late that afternoon, Sebastian spotted land. He saw the outline of Cape Ann to the west and hurried up to the bow to get a good view. The wind blew on his face as the *Funchal,* chasing the sun, got closer to Gloucester.

* * *

Birdie sat in the kitchen as Mama cleaned up after lunch. She could see the *bacalhau* on the counter and had a pretty good idea of what they would be having for dinner tomorrow.

"Where are we going today?" Winnie asked.

"I was thinking we could go to the beach at Bass Rocks and look at the big waves. How does that sound?"

"Super!" Winnie said.

"Well, go find your bonnet, and we'll set out."

"Have her home before dinner," Mama said to Birdie.

Birdie led her sister down the hill to the harbor. There was still a lot of storm damage to be cleaned up along the way. As they approached the historic Hotel Thorwald, Birdie told her sister about something she had read: "The newspaper said that three of the willow trees by the hotel came down during the storm."

"Oh, no, I loved those big trees," Winnie lamented.

"Yeah, me too," Birdie said.

When they arrived at the grand old hotel, with its beautiful red bricks and big tower overlooking the ocean, Birdie saw that the trees had already been hauled away. Winnie climbed up onto one of the stumps and faced out toward the ocean. She put her hands on her hips as she looked out at the waves. Birdie stood behind her and looked at the sea too. The waves, still large and impressive, crashed onto the rocks. She could see a pair of returning ships off in the distance.

"I wonder if one of those ships is Pa's," she said, pointing toward the two specks on the horizon. They were too far away for Birdie to make out any details, let alone the names of the ships.

\* \* \*

At the top of the Great Eastern Fishing Company building on Eastern Point, there was a watch tower named Crow's Nest. Its location on the wharf, between the sail-maker's shop and the ship chandlery, gave it an unobstructed view of the harbor, the bay, and out to sea. It was the perfect place to keep watch for returning ships from the fishing fleet.

Smokey Joe climbed the stairs to see who was on watch. Two men took turns to keep a constant watch whenever ships from the Gloucester fleet were down to the sea. They were paid if they spotted a ship and hoisted up a corresponding signal flag. It was important to the fishing industry to know when a fishing vessel was about to return with its perishable product, and it paid for that information well.

The man on the current watch kept his vigil in the small room at the top of the tower, looking through the wall of windows facing eastward. The room was filled with useful nautical instruments and aids, including charts, sextants, ship models, binoculars, telescopes, an azimuthal plate, and an aneroid barometer, as well as a box of signal flags, one for each ship in the fleet that was out at sea.

"You know, for a skipper who has retired, you spend a lot of time down at the wharf," the watchman said to Smokey Joe when he entered the room.

"That doesn't mean I'm looking to come out of retirement," Joe replied. "It's just that I find myself with a lot of time on my hands, and nothing interests me more than fishing and cribbage."

The watchman looked out the windows. He sat at the railing, on the only chair in the room, with his pipe in one hand and his binoculars in the other. As he watched he sang a classic Gloucester fishermen's song: "'Twas sou' sou'-west, then west sou'-west. From Rik-ie-vik to Gloucester; 'Twas strainin' sails and buried rails aboard the *Lucy Foster*—"

Abruptly he stopped singing. He had spotted two schooners on the horizon: a sixty-footer towing what looked to be a fifty-footer, or what was left of it. He noted the name of the first schooner. "*Funchal*," he said aloud.

Smokey Joe recognized the name, but she was not part of the Gloucester fleet. Then the watchman said, "*Dorcas*. We've been looking for you."

"That's Captain Silveira's schooner," Smokey Joe said.

The watchman grabbed the flag out of the box, and the two men went onto the balcony, where one of the local boys was loitering. "You there, run this up the pole, please," Smokey Joe said, handing the wharf rat a nickel while the watchman handed him the flag. The boy was more than happy to oblige; he had been waiting for just such an opportunity.

As he climbed up the rope ladder onto the roof to hoist the signal flag, the watchman ran down the stairs to report the news to the officer on duty at the fish company, who would then contact the owners of the ships, who would then contact the families of the skippers and the crews.

"I'd better call for an ambulance too, just in case," the watchman said, "and the newspapers."

Smokey Joe descended the stairs after the watchman and walked swiftly toward the harbor. He could see that many people had noticed the signal flag already. Within thirty minutes, the harbor would be abuzz as Gloucester awaited news of the *Dorcas*.

* * *

The *Funchal* arrived with the *Dorcas* at Pew's Wharf in Gloucester at half past three in the afternoon on Thursday. The *Funchal's* crew lashed the *Dorcas* to Frank Rose's schooner, the *Edith C. Rose*. Sebastian and his crew assisted.

*She made it back,* Sebastian thought as he worked. *What a great little sworder.*

"Pass a line," Captain Sears instructed his crew. "Pull her alongside."

The crew maneuvered what was left of the little sworder into place, so that she was firmly secured to the starboard rail of the *Edith C. Rose*. Then the crews of both schooners disembarked.

Sebastian shook hands with Captain Sears vigorously. "Thanks again, Captain Sears."

"He was a good man," the older skipper replied.

The rest of the crew of the *Dorcas* all added their thanks before the captain departed.

The next thing Sebastian had to do was make sure that Brown got medical attention. The crew had bandaged his face and Doc had stitched him up, but his leg was so twisted that he couldn't even walk.

Once Brown was in the hands of the local ambulance company, Sebastian met briefly with Captain Fronteiro, to tell him what had happened to the *Dorcas* and to Joseph.

The crew then unloaded the thirteen swordfish. By that time the buzz at the wharf had turned into a frenzy. The news had spread through town about the fate of the schooner.

Domingoes still had one more task to perform. Sebastian watched as the striker grabbed a hatchet and a knife to remove his harpoons and his horseshoe from their makeshift steering system. Retrieving his good-luck charm, Domingoes tucked it again under his belt.

When the mob had dispersed, all the swordfish were weighed. By then Captain Fronteiro had all the information he needed from Sebastian to pay the crew. Those who had stuck around would be paid cash on demand. Domingoes had waited to receive his pay, one and a quarter share. It came to only thirteen dollars, all of which would be donated to Our Lady of Good Voyage as "God's share."

Domingoes looked disappointed. His new lay, on a good trip, would have been nearer to a hundred dollars.

"Sorry, Domingoes," Sebastian said. "This was more than just a broken trip." He wondered how much beef and cabbage thirteen dollars could buy.

"Sorry about the skipper," the striker replied. "He was one of the greatest Gloucestermen."

They both considered themselves fortunate to be still breathing.

Domingoes started walking up toward his home on Portuguese Hill, carrying his ash-wood harpoons parallel to the ground, his whalecraft bag strung over his left shoulder. Pulling out his horseshoe, he called back to Sebastian, "At least I still have this, and my beloved Rosella."

Before Sebastian left the *Dorcas*, he agreed to do one interview with a reporter from the local newspaper. He described the schooner's departure from Gloucester the week before, and his brother's uneasy feeling. He told the reporter about their arrival at Georges Bank, how they had fished with success through Monday, and their chance meeting with the *Funchal*. He explained how, early on Tuesday, the barometer had predicted the oncoming storm, and how they had followed their sail plan until tragedy befell his brother. He then described the miracle of the three crew-members climbing back aboard, and how they had righted the ship and gotten the motor going again, and the alternate steering method. He continued the story up until the current moment, and then he said grimly, "The worst of it is that now I've got to break the news to my brother's wife and children."

Without another word, he started to walk toward the hill. Then he felt a hand on his arm—it was his nephew. They hugged each other. "Now I understand *saudade*," Silva said.

"Yeah," Sebastian sighed.

They parted ways. Silva went home to his young bride, while Sebastian grabbed his sou'wester hat and his brother's log book and poetry journal, and walked away from the harbor.

He could see signs for National Defense Day everywhere as he walked up the hill toward his older brother's house. When he arrived at the white Victorian house, he stood still for a moment, collecting his thoughts.

Winnie was hanging over the front gate, using it as a

makeshift swing set. She looked at him curiously as she swung back and forth, her shoes banging the fence. He passed her, walked up the front steps, and went through the front door. Ahead of him was the main stairwell of the house. He turned right into the parlor, where his sister-in-law Mary was sitting in a high-backed wing chair.

She stood up, and they locked eyes for a second. Sebastian didn't speak at first; he just wrung his yellow sou'wester hat nervously. "Mary—" he began.

No more words were needed. Mary screamed and fainted.

# The Fisherman

I sit beside Lethean streams,
And in, that ghostly tangle
Of quaint and ill-assorted dreams
Fantastically angle.

The wand of memory is my rod,
My hook is old affection,
With which I keep extracting odd
Phantoms of recollection.

The creatures glisten in the wave
And magically quiver;
But, once ashore, what charm they have
Is apt to fade forever.

And yet the future is so dark
And grimly unalluring
That I fish on, and scarce remark
The failures I'm securing.

*The Fisherman,* Gamaliel Bradford

*Sunday, August 23, 1925.*

The night after the *Dorcas* returned, Captain Ambrose Smith of the *Mary H.* of New Bedford, out at sea east of Sankaty Head, thought he heard the sound of a foghorn. The horn blew in a series of long sustained blasts, and this allowed him to get a bearing on the distress signal. Finally he spotted the *Alice and Wilson.* Captain Hall and his crew's luck had finally changed for the better.

After they were towed back to Gloucester, they unloaded the thirty swordfish they had caught. The fish fetched a good price: as a result of the storm, there was a widespread shortage of fresh fish in Gloucester and Boston.

Shortly after this, the schooner *Christie A. Cox* also arrived safely in Gloucester, thanks to the heroic actions of her skipper, Captain Brown.

Meanwhile, all of the available search-and-rescue ships continued to patrol the fishing grounds, looking for signs of the missing ships. The *Protector* steamed north toward Sable Island. Down by Georges Bank, the Coast Guard cutter *Ossipee* found a buoy with the letters "A&W" painted on it. Not far away, the beam trawler *Ocean* found a yellow dory marked with the name "Murley".

The final piece of good news about the fleet arrived when the *Herbert Parker,* commanded by John Carrancho, returned to Gloucester. She had been fishing far offshore, at the Sable Island fishing grounds, and though she had lost all fourteen of her dories, the entire crew had survived. Once back in Gloucester, they began repairs immediately, while their cargo of 180,000 pounds of salted fish was unloaded.

\* \* \*

It had been a tragic year for the Gloucester fleet since the August Gale. Back in December, John F. Ryan from the *Elizabeth and Ruth* was lost when his dory was swamped. A few weeks later, in January, Henry Colt was washed overboard from the *Commonwealth*. Later that same week, Seymour Cochran and Thomas Hosdon, out dory-fishing, decided to row back to the *John J. Fallon,* but the schooner didn't see them and inadvertently rammed them. Hosdon was able to grab onto the bowsprit stay, but Cochran sank into the deep forever. A few days later, on the *Elk*, Anselme Hubbard and Reuben Melanson were also lost while dory-fishing: a blinding snow storm emerged on Brown's Bank, and the two men and their dory were never found again. That same week, during a different January gale, two Gloucestermen from the haddocking fleet were lost up at LeHave: Eli Goodick was washed overboard from the *Oretha F. Spinney* while on watch, and Jarvis Meuse, out in his dory, never returned to the *Gov. Marshall*. In early April, two men from the schooner *Hesperus* were hauling their trawls when their dory overturned in a squall: Howard Carew drowned, but his dory mate, Patrick Burke, managed to hold on for an hour and a half. He was unconscious but alive when his crew-mates found him. In May, Lin Woolf from the schooner *Elise* disappeared from his dory out on Brown's Bank. A few weeks later, Thomas Fraser from the *Elizabeth W. Nunan* also disappeared from his dory while hauling trawls.

\* \* \*

One year after the events of August 1924, the City of Gloucester prepared for the dedication of the Gloucester Fishermen's statue, the conclusion to the celebration of their three hundredth anniversary.

At three o'clock in the afternoon, Sebastian, Bella, Olga, and Alice arrived at the Cut with Joseph's widow, Mary, and her three youngest daughters. Sebastian's second youngest niece, Kiddo, was dressed in her Girl Scout uniform.

He spoke with all of the crew-members of the *Dorcas,* as well as countless supportive friends and family, as they gathered for the ceremony. About five thousand members of the Gloucester and Cape Ann community attended, wearing their finest summer suits and dresses and wide-brimmed summer hats. Among them were Joseph Silva and his young bride, Julia. Together the extended family walked toward Stacey Boulevard to find a good spot for watching the unveiling.

Julia was wearing her best summer outfit, a white knitted shirt with a powder-blue coat and a matching pleated skirt, hat, and umbrella. "What was that Portuguese word you learned during the storm?" she asked her husband.

"*Saudade*," Silva replied. "*Saudade*," he said once more with a sigh.

Sebastian heard the exchange.

Then Doc and Merico appeared. "It's the perfect time of year for this ceremony," Merico said to the group. "All the roses and dahlias are in bloom, which is good for making the bouquets. The days are warm and dry, and the ebb tide is about go out, which will help with the dedication service when people scatter their flowers."

Brown and Murray were the next two crew-members to join the group. Brown was still walking with an abnormal gait from his leg injury, which had never fully healed.

Soon afterward Sebastian saw Domingoes approaching with his wife, Rosella; both stood out in the crowd because of their height. Many of the men nearby looked at Rosella; Sebastian wasn't the only Gloucesterman who thought she was the most beautiful woman in the city.

Tone was the last crew-member of the *Dorcas* to arrive. He joined Sebastian's family and the rest of the crew in front of the statue, right before the ceremony started.

Then Captain Fronteiro and his wife walked by, stopping to shake hands with Sebastian and the crew before getting in line to talk to Joseph's widow.

* * *

Smokey Joe walked with his family along Stacey Boulevard. They met Captain Hall and the crew of the schooner *Alice and Wilson*. Smokey Joe knew Captain Hall and had heard about the tragic incidents of the August Gale last summer. He had never met James Holland, Joaquim Dores, or Manuel Marques, but he had already heard their tale.

Next his family encountered Captain Blackburn. The two men acknowledged each other with nods as they passed each other.

"I'm just glad your name is not on the wall," Mary Mesquita said to her husband, referring to the memorial wall behind them.

"Yes, and I intend to keep it that way by staying retired," Smokey Joe replied.

"Was there ever a time out at sea when you thought you wouldn't make it back?" Mary Dahlmer asked her father.

"September 1907 was pretty bad," Smokey Joe said. "Fourteen men went into the water during that gale, while they were fishing for Captain Silva. I thought it was folly of them to launch dories in that squall. We found four of them and pulled them aboard the *Frances P. Mesquita*, but the other ten men are on the wall behind us. I'm glad we didn't launch our dories. I never understood why Captain Silva allowed it that day, in that kind of weather."

"When were you most terrified at sea?" his daughter asked.

"When we ran into the German U-boat during the Great War," he said, not needing any time to think. "We didn't see it coming at first. We were out fishing near Sable Island, the graveyard of the Atlantic. It was in August of 1918, right before that terrible Spanish Flu outbreak. I had seen the French trawler *Triumph* on the horizon, and I knew Captain Pierre. I would usually check in with him and see if he had any mail to be sent. So we pulled up beside them. 'Hey, George, have you been busy?' I called. 'Did you get any fish?' We didn't realize anything was amiss until they fired two warning shots over our bow.

"Then we heard a loud German voice shouting at us through a megaphone. 'Heave to, we're going to sink your vessel,' the voice told us. They had us at gunpoint. Then their captain told us to row over and come aboard with our papers. There's something about those Germans, always wanting to see your papers…

"They let us row back afterward to get some supplies, but two large German men, dressed in black, came with us. They carried guns and a large black bag. One of my crew told me later that he had recently seen those same Huns in Oscar LeVeau's bar room back in Gloucester. I guess they'd been doing some reconnaissance. They allowed us to pack up some bread and water and launch the dories.

"Then they pulled a bomb out of the black bag and put it on

the *Francis J. Ohara*. A minute after we'd pulled away from her, the bomb exploded and she split in two and sank. We rowed for the mainland for four whole days until we were rescued by another schooner. And so we didn't end up on the wall."

"Did you know any of the men who will be memorialized today?" his daughter asked.

"Yes, many of them. But I knew Captain Silveira the best. He was a member of the Master Mariners' Association, like me. We fished together often, and he wasn't half terrible at cribbage."

They passed Captain Doyle, who was surrounded by an entourage of people all engrossed by a story he was telling: "It was a sea serpent, I tell you! I saw it with my own two eyes. It had a head like an eel, and it was a hundred and thirty feet long, longer than my boat even." Very few of the crowd believed him, but they all enjoyed the story.

Smokey Joe and his family walked on, and soon they reached the Silveira family. The retired skipper shook hands with Sebastian. "How are you holding up these days, my old friend?" Smokey Joe asked.

"I'm doing well, all things considered," Sebastian said. "I'm staying focused on my family and my daughters' futures."

"Are you going to try to become a Master Mariner?"

"To be honest, I haven't been out to sea since that gale. I've been learning as much as I can about radio telegraphy instead. How about you? Are you still planning to come out of retirement?"

"Let's just say that ship has sailed," Smokey Joe said,

garnering a glance of approval from his wife. "So both of us have now swallowed the anchor for good."

"It would appear so. What will you do next?" Sebastian asked.

"I'm thinking about going down to Washington and trying my hand at becoming a lobbyist," Smokey Joe said, to Sebastian's surprise. "Someone needs to start advocating for the fishermen of Gloucester. And besides, I want to give that President Coolidge a piece of my mind for not showing up today for the unveiling."

* * *

Mary stood with her family and received everyone's good wishes. A line of people waited their turn to let her know that she had been in their thoughts and prayers. She stood in a stalwart posture, still dressed in black, as she had been every day since Sebastian had brought the news about her husband.

She had also been given a fish every day since then—a thoughtful gesture from the Gloucester Fishermen's Institute. Every day one of the fishermen from the institute would deliver the fish to her house. Many of these men were here today to be part of the ceremony.

Chaplain George E. Russell, the president of the Fishermen's Institute, was the first in line to talk to her.

"Thanks so much for stopping by, Chaplain," Mary said.

"Well, of course, Mrs. Silveira. I must say you're looking well. I hope the fish we've been sending were helpful."

"Yes, indeed. I can't thank you enough. It's been most

thoughtful of the Institute."

"It's the least we could do," the Chaplain said. He offered her some personal memories and reflections about Joseph, providing Mary with much-needed comfort. Then he excused himself, as he had many duties to attend to for the unveiling.

The next person in the queue was Captain Fronteiro. He also told Mary some lighthearted stories and paid his respects to her.

Near the end of the line was Captain Blackburn. "Your Joseph was one of the great ones, Mrs. Silveira," he said to her. "He truly was one of the greatest highliners in the Gloucester fleet."

Mary listened to him extolling her husband, who had been his close friend, but one part of her mind was wondering where Birdie was. It wasn't like her oldest daughter to be late for an important event.

"So will you be departing soon on a new adventure?" Mary asked the captain. "Another trip to England or Portugal?"

"Not likely, Mrs. Silveira. Between you and me, I've decided to give up those long solo trips. I'm getting too old for them. Instead I'm going to keep to my tavern and be thankful that I still have my soft-drink license."

"That sounds like a wise decision, Captain Blackburn," Mary said.

The final person in the line was Smokey Joe. He kept their conversation bright and cheerful, and Mary appreciated that. First he told her about a strange winter trip he had taken with her husband. "It was in the winter of 1907, when we had a strange warm spell. The weather was so mild that Captain Silveira and I ended up fishing in short-sleeved shirts—in the middle of winter, if you can believe that!" Then he told a few more lighthearted stories about Joseph.

At last Mary said, "Thanks for all your thoughts and prayers, Captain Mesquita." She was probably the only person in Gloucester who didn't refer to him by his nickname.

By now the ceremony was about to start. Mary stood patiently, thinking long and hard about her lot in life as a fisherman's wife.

\* \* \*

The seventeen survivors from the sinking of the *Republic* in February of 1925 were in attendance at the unveiling, honoring Captain Peter Dunsky and their crew-mate Samuel Cole. They had been out halibut-fishing a few miles from Seal Island in Nova Scotia. During a thunderstorm that severely limited their visibility, an unidentified three-masted schooner crashed into the *Republic*. Many of the crew were washed overboard during the collision, but all of them made it back to the *Republic* except for the skipper and Cole. The schooner that had run them down disappeared and was not seen again. The seventeen survivors had to abandon ship but were able to make it to the Cape Sable Island life-saving station in three dories.

At the outer edge of the crowd stood the nine survivors of the schooner *Rex*, which had been lost earlier that summer, in June. She had been halibut-fishing at the banks of Quero, east of Sable Island. She had anchored in a heavy morning fog. At about nine o'clock, the nine men were topside on watch. They blew their foghorn frequently and heard nothing back in return. The other fifteen people—including Captain Thomas O. Downie; the cook, Austin Firth; and his ten-year-old son Charles—were below in their bunks or in the forecastle. The boy was on his first ever fishing trip with his father. He had been looking forward to it all year. Suddenly a large black hull emerged from the fog. The Cunard Anchor line steamship *Tuscania* rammed straight through the *Rex*. The nine men topside all jumped overboard before the impact, but the fifteen below were not so lucky. They clawed like rats to escape, but the force of the impact was too much. The *Rex* foundered, and they descended into their watery graves. The *Tuscania* rang her bells and turned about to search for survivors, but amid the flotsam they found only the nine men who had been topside.

Many other crews from many other vessels, along with their friends and families and nearly all of the tight-knit community of Gloucester, formed the large crowd who had gathered to honor the forty-five souls whose names were to be read aloud that day. Twelve of them were from the gale in August of the previous year, and fifteen were from the wreck of the *Rex*.

* * *

Sebastian recognized Andrew Larsen as he emerged from the crowd, wearing a dark suit. Sebastian had heard the tale; he knew Larsen was there to honor the memory of his brother and his uncle, as well as the memory of the man who had gone down to sea in his place, Hilary Conrad, and the rest of the crew of the *Anita and Bernice L.* All of them had been lost in the August Gale, after Andrew, with unexplainable intuition, had decided at the last minute not to go on that fateful fishing trip.

They shook hands. "That was a terrible storm," Sebastian said. "We both lost a brother, but we ought to be thankful that our names won't be read today."

Larsen agreed and continued on his way.

Sebastian and his family waited for one last family-member to arrive. He wondered where Birdie was and why she was running late. Finally he saw his niece in the crowd. She was easy to spot, thanks to the man she was with. He was over six feet tall, with short dark hair and a handlebar mustache, and they made for a striking couple thanks to their height difference. Sebastian liked Birdie's fiancé, a man she had met at college. His name was Philip Reep. Like Birdie, he was a talented music student at the Eastman School. They said their hellos to everyone else in the family, then stopped in front of Sebastian.

"Hello, uncle, nice to see you," Birdie said. "You remember my fiancé, Philip?"

"Of course. Thanks for coming, Philip," Sebastian said.

Now that his whole family had arrived, Sebastian could focus his attention on the unveiling ceremony. Mayor Carleton H. Parsons, who was also president of the Tercentenary Permanent Memorial Association, commenced the ceremony. "It is with great pride," he began, "that I stand here in front of all of you, to open this most historic ceremony. Look behind me to Stage Fort Park on the harbor side. This was the site of our fair city's first settlement. Ever since then, the brave men of Gloucester and Cape Ann have gone down to the sea in ships. They know the risks and the perils, and yet they fish on. We have tremendous gratitude for the men and women who have given us this wonderful boulevard, and now this new grand monument. Ladies and gentlemen, let us all welcome the statue of this stalwart helmsman."

After the mayor concluded his opening remarks, the band performed the song "My Own America." Then Reverend E. Milton Grant said a prayer in honor of the hardy fisherman of Gloucester, and the band played "One Fleeting Hour."

Captain John A. MacKinnon prepared to unveil the statue, waiting for the signal from the mayor. The band played "America" and Captain MacKinnon pulled the rope. The veil fell off the eight-foot bronze statue on its square granite base.

Sebastian and his family and his crew were in front of the statue when it was unveiled. He looked at the bronze helmsman bravely holding onto the wheel as he steered and remembered his last glimpse of Joseph on the *Dorcas*. He had been standing to the right side of the wheel box at the helm, just like this old salt, with both hands on the wheel.

"Someday," Winnie said beside him, "that statue of Pa will become patina."

The former mayor, William A. MacInnis, was the next dignitary to speak at the ceremony. He recited Longfellow's poem "The Secret of the Sea" to the crowd:

"Ah! What pleasant visions haunt me as I gaze upon the sea!

All the old romantic legends, all my dreams, come back to me.

"Sails of silk and ropes of sandal, such as gleam in ancient lore; and the singing of the sailors, and the answer from the shore!

"How he heard the ancient helmsman chant a song so wild and clear, that the sailing sea-bird slowly poised upon the mast to hear.

"Till his soul was full of longing, and he cried, with impulse strong,— 'Helmsman! for the love of heaven, teach me, too, that wondrous song!'

"'Wouldst thou,' — so the helmsman answered, 'Learn the secrets of the sea? Only those who brave its dangers comprehend its mystery!'"

Then Mayor MacInnis paused and then delivered his speech, which he seemed to address to the statue itself. "Welcome! Fishermen-Friend — thrice welcome home to your city whose name you have made so glorious. Stay with us on this stern and rock-bound coast, and guard our harbor always.

"Oft in the stilly night, you will bid good-bye to Gloucester men leaving home and harbor for the fishing banks and after a season you will welcome them returning—yes, even on the wings of a storm.

"Through it all you will be calm, courageous and confident because you have behind you a heritage reaching back to the days of the fishermen of Galilee.

"Disciplined by three centuries of toil in wringing a livelihood from the depths of the ocean, in you faith has found an abiding place, for you have seen the works of the Lord and his wonders in the deep.

"You have lived worthily, and with purpose, exemplifying patriotism, diligence in business, and the nobility of labor. You are and will be the inspiration of generations of people to whom your wholesome courage and vigorous manhood will be guide and stay o'er life's tempestuous sea.

"Gloucester is fair, yes, wondrous fair, for artists' brush and poets' pen but still her worth, beyond compare is in her race of sturdy men."

The band played Handel's "Largo" as six wreaths were left in front of the statue. The throng started to move as the mayor concluded the dedication. It was now time for the roll of the dead. Sebastian and his family got ready to join the procession.

* * *

Birdie and Philip were at the front of the crowd that walked slowly over to the Blynman Bridge. They stopped at the Cut, each holding a bouquet of roses and dahlias. Reverend G. Bennet Van Buskirk offered a prayer, and John Jacobson played a cornet solo of "The Lost Chord." The choir from the Methodist church sang a hymn written by a local songwriter named Mary Brooks. Birdie and Philip sang along:

"Scatter flowers on the waves; there our fathers found their graves, brothers, sons and husbands sleep; strew your garlands o'er the deep.

"Ebbing tide of summer day, bear these blossoms on their

way, north and east to bank and coast, where they lie whom we love most.

"He who marks each secret spot, Christ who shared a fisher's lot— He will guard each wave-washed bed till the sea gives up its dead."

Then Birdie listened as Chaplain Russell read the roll of the dead, forty-five Gloucester sailors and fishermen who had been lost at sea over the past year. As he read each name, a member of the local Girl Scout troop tossed a bouquet of flowers into the canal.

"Eldridge Corkum," the chaplain said. "George A. Stubert. Antonio Santos Cortina. Duarte Magellers. Manuel Natario. Captain Joseph F. Silveira."

Kiddo dropped her bouquet into the canal, in memory of Pa. Her curly red hair glowed in the bright August summer sun.

"James Holland. Joaquim V. Dores. Manuel Marques. Captain Albert Larsen. Edward M. Proctor. Fritz Mann. Peter Nelson. Joseph Targett. Charles Larsen. Alvin Selig. Hilary Conrad. John F. Ryan. Eli Goodick. Jarvis Meuse. Henry Colt. Anselme Hubbard. Reuben Melanson. Howard Carew. Harry Baker. Thomas Fraser. Lin Woolf. Seymour Cochran. Captain Peter Dunsky. Samuel Cole. Captain Thomas O. Downie. George Johnson. Joseph Dalton. Angus D. McDonald. Angus Smith. Clyde Larkin. Samuel Tibbetts. Charles Goodick. William Roach. William Turner. Archie Hill. Oscar Williams. Charles Wieball. Austin Firth. Charles Austin Firth."

The final Girl Scout dropped the last bouquet of roses and dahlias in honor of the boy who had been the youngest victim of the

August Gale, then stepped back into the throng.

"In memory of all the seamen, who through all the years, have found a last resting place in the waters that wash every shore, we lovingly strew these flowers." Chaplain Russell said.

Many members of the crowd followed suit, tossing additional bouquets into the canal. Le and Winnie dropped in their flowers, followed by Birdie and Philip. The ebb tide carried the flowers out to sea while the band played taps.

Afterward Birdie and Philip walked back to his automobile on Stacey Boulevard. Birdie hummed the tune to "Scatter Flowers on the Waves." She thought about how hard life had been in these past few years, with the war, the Spanish Flu, and—worst of all for her family—the August Gale. But time had started to heal her wounds, and now she felt a renewed optimism for the future.

"You know, I just came up with an idea," she said to her fiancé. "What if we started an opera company that sang all the songs in English? It would be the first of its kind. The first of its kind in all of America."

# Acknowledgments

Thanks to my father, and to my family, for passing down the oral history about my great-grandfather, Captain Joseph Silveira, and the swordfishing schooner *Dorcas*. That family folklore served as the primary inspiration for this book.

This book happened because of librarians. I can't express enough gratitude to the Sawyer Free Library in Gloucester. So much of this story was based on newspaper articles found in the microfilm copies of the *Gloucester Daily Times and Cape Ann Advertiser* from 1924 to 1925. Thanks to the very patient research staff, I finally understand the difference between microfiche and microfilm (I think).

Thanks to Brendan Keohane for designing an incredible book cover.

Thanks to GrubStreet in Boston for introducing me to the craft of writing, and thanks in particular to my instructors: Olivia Kate Cerrone, Ursula DeYoung, Christine Pride, David J. Sciuto, Timothy Weed and Carolyn Zaikowski, who all helped me hone that craft. And a very special thanks to Ursula DeYoung, who was not only one of my GrubStreet instructors, but also my line editor.

If you are interested in researching the rich maritime history of Gloucester, I highly recommend checking in with the Maritime Gloucester Education Center. Their local schooner expert knew about the *Dorcas,* and he graciously showed me numerous models of similar schooners up in the Gorton's Seafoods Gallery.

*The Perfect Storm* by Sebastian Junger was the cornerstone literary inspiration for this book. Coincidently, my great-grandfather's name is engraved on the same exact tablet at the Fishermen's Memorial as the crew from the *Andrea Gail*, along with all the rest of the victims from the August Gale. Another great Gloucester themed book I would recommend is the *Gloucester Fishermen's Wives Cookbook* by Susan Pollack.

There are numerous other authors who have provided me with inspiration about Gloucester, such as: Linda Greenlaw, Joseph E. Garland, James B. Connolly and Rudyard Kipling. I also recommend the tales about swordfishing by Hemmingway and Zane Grey.

In addition to those literary influences, I also want to mention some of the important films that provided me some inspiration. A great film influence was the Elmer Clifton 1922 silent film *Down to the Sea in Ships*, which featured the real life whaling bark *Wanderer*, just a few years before her wreckage during the August Gale of 1924. *The Age of Swordfish* by Vittorio De Seta was an interesting 1954 black and white documentary about swordfishing in Sicily. Lastly, I recommend *The Last Whalers* by William Neufeld, a 1969 documentary which showed a pretty stark portrayal of sperm whaling on the island of Pico.

Big thanks to my cousins Suzi and Tina for maintaining such a detailed family tree, which I referred to many times to fact check some of the family details in the story, and thanks also for being beta readers of one of the early versions of my manuscript.

Lastly, I would be totally remiss if I didn't give a huge call out to Roberta Sheedy for all the effort she put into her website, *Out of Gloucester*. It is a virtual tome and treasure trove of Gloucester maritime historical heritage, and I highly recommend it to anyone who is doing research about their family's connection to Gloucester's rich and storied history, as "the oldest active seaport in the United States".

# Bibliography

"Abandon Hope for Sworder." *Gloucester Daily Times and Cape Ann Advertiser*. September 18, 1924.

"Abandon Hope for the Murley." *Gloucester Daily Times and Cape Ann Advertiser*. September 19, 1924.

Abbe, Cleveland. *Monthly Weather Review*. Volume XXVII. Atlantic Oceanographic & Meteorological Laboratory (AOML). National Oceanic & Atmospheric Administration (NOAA). August, 1899.

Alves, Eugene (Rev.), Interviewee and Masters, David, Interviewer. "Toward an Oral History of Cape Ann: Alves, Eugene (Rev.)." *Sawyer Free Library*. Gloucester, MA. 1978.

Anderson, Edith, Interviewee and Masters, David, Interviewer. "Toward an Oral History of Cape Ann: Anderson, Edith." *Sawyer Free Library*. Gloucester, MA. 1978.

"Another Hit by Heavy Sea." *Gloucester Daily Times and Cape Ann Advertiser*. September 2, 1924.

"Another Sworder Brings Grim Tale." *Gloucester Daily Times and Cape Ann Advertiser*. August 30, 1924.

"Anxiety over Fleet Subsides." *Gloucester Daily Times and Cape Ann Advertiser*. September 2, 1924.

Ashe, Thomas. *History of the Azores or Western Islands; Containing an Account of the Government, Laws and Religion, the Manners, Ceremonies, and*

*Character of the Inhabitants*. Sherwood, Neely and Jones, Paternoster Row. London. 1813.

"Attended Mass in Oil Skins to Keep Promise." *Gloucester Daily Times and Cape Ann Advertiser*. September 10, 1924.

Bachelder, Peter Dow and Smith, Mason Philip. *Four Short Blasts — The Gale of 1898 and the Loss of the Steamer Portland*. The Provincial Press. Portland, ME. 2003.

Baer, Chris. "This Was Then: The Augusta — The Hurricane of 1924 Took its Toll." *MV Times*. March 2, 2017.

Baird, Edwin, Ed. *Weird Tales the Unique Magazine*. Rural Publishing Corp. Indianapolis, IN. Volume 1. Number 1. March 1923.

——. *Weird Tales the Unique Magazine*. Rural Publishing Corp. Indianapolis, IN. Volume 1. Number 2. April 1923.

——. *Weird Tales the Unique Magazine*. Rural Publishing Corp. Indianapolis, IN. Volume 1. Number 3. May 1923.

——. *Weird Tales the Unique Magazine*. Rural Publishing Corp. Indianapolis, IN. Volume 1. Number 4. June 1923.

——. *Weird Tales the Unique Magazine*. Rural Publishing Corp. Indianapolis, IN. Volume II. Number 1. July-August 1923.

——. *Weird Tales the Unique Magazine*. Rural Publishing Corp. Indianapolis, IN. Volume II. Number 2. September 1923.

——. *Weird Tales the Unique Magazine*. Rural Publishing Corp. Indianapolis, IN. Volume II. Number 3. October 1923.

———. *Weird Tales the Unique Magazine*. Rural Publishing Corp. Indianapolis, IN. Volume 2. Number 1. November 1923.

———. *Weird Tales the Unique Magazine*. Rural Publishing Corp. Indianapolis, IN. Volume 3. Number 1. December 1923 – January 1924.

———. *Weird Tales the Unique Magazine*. Rural Publishing Corp. Indianapolis, IN. Volume 3. Number 2. February 1924.

———. *Weird Tales the Unique Magazine*. Rural Publishing Corp. Indianapolis, IN. Volume 3. Number 3. March 1924.

———. *Weird Tales the Unique Magazine*. Rural Publishing Corp. Indianapolis, IN. Volume 4. Number 1. April 1924.

———. *Weird Tales the Unique Magazine*. Rural Publishing Corp. Indianapolis, IN. Volume 4. Number 2. May, June, July 1924.

"Bark Wanderer Lost." *Vineyard Gazette*. August 26, 1924.

Barron, Grace., Brayton, Linda, Interviewer, and Masters, David, Interviewer. "Toward an Oral History of Cape Ann: Barron, Grace." *Sawyer Free Library*. Gloucester, MA. 1978.

Bartlett, Kim. *The Finest Kind – The Fishermen of Gloucester*. W W Norton & Company, Inc. New York, NY. 1977.

Battaglia, Pietro, *et al.* "Evolution , Crisis, and New Scenarios of the Italian Swordfish Harpoon Fishery." *Regional Studies in Marine Science*. Volume 21. May 2018.

Braithwaite, William Stanley ed. *Anthology of Magazine Verse for 1924 and Yearbook of American Poetry*. B.J, Brimmer Company. Boston, MA. 1924.

Brooks, Alfred Mansfield. *Gloucester Recollected - A Familiar History.* Cape Ann Historical Association. 1974.

"Captain Mesquita, Fisherman, Dead." *The New York Times.* November 10, 1933.

"Captains of Bay State Fishing Fleets No. 13. Captain Joseph P. Mesquita." *The Boston Globe.* December 13, 1909.

Coggswell, John F. "The Fishermen's Race." *Popular Mechanics.* October, 1931.

Coleridge, Samuel Taylor. *The Rime of the Ancient Mariner.* Dover Publications, Inc. New York, NY. 1970.

Connolly, James B. *The Book of the Gloucester Fishermen.* The John Day Company. New York, NY. 1930.

———. *The Deep Sea's Toll.* Charles Scribner's Sons. New York, NY. 1905.

———. *Gloucestermen: Stories of the Fishing Fleet.* Charles Scribner's Sons. New York, NY. 1930.

———. *Out of Gloucester.* Charles Scribner's Sons. New York, NY. 1906.

———. *The Port of Gloucester.* Doubleday, Doran & Company, Inc. New York, NY. 1940.

———. *The Seiners.* Charles Scribner's Sons. New York, NY. 1905.

Costa, Natacha. *Whaling Tradition of the Azores.* Itinari. August 2018.

"Crew of Beam Trawler Encounter Sea Serpent." *Gloucester Daily Times and Cape Ann Advertiser.* May 27, 1925.

"Cutters to Aid Fishermen." *The New York Times.* August 31, 1924.

Dahlmer, Mary, Interviewee and Masters, David, Interviewer. "Toward an Oral History of Cape Ann: Dahlmer, Mary." *Sawyer Free Library.* Gloucester, MA. 1978.

Day, W. P. "Tropical Disturbances During the Hurricane Season of 1924." *Monthly Weather Review.* Atlantic Oceanographic & Meteorological Laboratory (AOML). National Oceanic & Atmospheric Administration (NOAA).

"Defense Day and What it Means." *Gloucester Daily Times and Cape Ann Advertiser.* August 29, 1924.

"A Defense Day Proclamation." *Gloucester Daily Times and Cape Ann Advertiser.* August 26, 1924.

Domingos, Manuel P., Jr, Interviewee, Brayton, Linda, Interviewer. and Masters, David, Interviewer, "Toward an Oral History of Cape Ann: Domingos, Manuel P. Jr." *Sawyer Free Library.* Gloucester, MA. 1978.

"Drowned on Georges while Hauling Trawls." *Gloucester Daily Times and Cape Ann Advertiser.* May 23, 1925.

Eells, Elsie Spicer. *The Islands of Magic – Legends, Folk and Fairy Tales from the Azores.* Theophania Publishing. Lexington, KY. 2015.

"Eight of Whaler's Crew are Missing." *Gloucester Daily Times and Cape*

*Ann Advertiser*. August 27, 1924.

"Elaborate Plans for Defense Day." *Gloucester Daily Times and Cape Ann Advertiser*. August 22, 1924.

Eliot, T. S. *The Waste Land*. Harcourt Brace & Company. New York, NY. 1997.

"Elk Arrives with Flag Half-Mast." *Gloucester Daily Times and Cape Ann Advertiser*. January 29, 1925.

"Elks and Friends Danced at the Beach." *Gloucester Daily Times and Cape Ann Advertiser*. August 22, 1924.

Ellis, Richard. *Swordfish – A Biography of the Ocean Gladiator*. The University of Chicago Press. Chicago & London. 2013.

Eustis, Harry, Interviewee, Brayton, Linda, Interviewer, and Masters, David, Interviewer. "Toward an Oral History of Cape Ann: Eustis, Harry." *Sawyer Free Library*. Gloucester, MA. 1978.

Fifield, Charles Woodbury Jr. *Along the Gloucester Waterfront 1938 to 1946*. Eagle Printing Company. Northbridge, MA. 2001.

"Fifteen Perished when Liner Rammed Local Halibut Craft." *Gloucester Daily Times and Cape Ann Advertiser*. June 29, 1925.

*Fifty-Sixth Annual List of Merchant Vessels of the United States*. Department of Commerce Bureau of Navigation. Government Printing Office. Washington, D.C. June 30, 1924.

"Find Dory of Missing Man." *Gloucester Daily Times and Cape Ann Advertiser*. May 6, 1925.

"Find No Trace of Distressed Craft on Banks." *Gloucester Daily Times and Cape Ann Advertiser.* September 4, 1924.

"Fisherman Lost Life When Craft Rammed Dory." *Gloucester Daily Times and Cape Ann Advertiser.* January 20, 1925.

*Fishermen of the Atlantic.* Fishing Master's Association Inc. Boston, MA. 1924.

*Fishermen's Ballads, and Songs of the Sea.* Procter Brothers, Publishers. Gloucester, MA. 1874.

*Fishermen's Own Book* Procter Brothers, Publishers. Gloucester, MA. 1882.

Freud, Sigmund, McLintock, David, and Haughton, Hugh. *The Uncanny.* Penguin Books. New York, NY. 2003.

"Gale-Lashed Arabic Docks with 75 Hurt; 4 Other Liners Hit." *The New York Times.* Thursday, August 28, 1924.

Garland, Joseph E. *Adventure: Last of the Great Gloucester Dory-Fishing Schooners.* The Curious Traveler Press. Gloucester, MA. 2000.

——. *Down to the Sea: The Fishing Schooners of Gloucester.* David R Godine Publisher Inc. Jaffrey, NY. 1983.

——. *Eastern Point.* Noone House. Peterborough, NH. 1971.

——. *The Gloucester Guide – A Retrospective Ramble.* Gloucester 350th Anniversary Celebration, Inc. 1973.

——. *Gloucester on the Wind - America's Greatest Fishing Port in the Days of Sail.* Arcadia Publishing. Charleston, SC. 1995.

————. *Lone Voyager – The Extraordinary Adventures of Howard Blackburn, Hero Fisherman of Gloucester.* Simon & Schuster. New York, NY. 2000.

Giambarba, Paul. *Whales, Whaling and Whalecraft.* Scrimshaw Publishing. Centerville, MA. 1967.

"Gloucester Band Leader Dead at Age of 91 Years." *Gloucester Daily Times and Cape Ann Advertiser.* August 23, 1924.

*Gloucester Master Mariners' Association Yearbook.* Gloucester, MA. Master Mariners' Association. 1925.

Goncalves, Joseph L, Interviewee and Master, David, Interviewer. "Toward an Oral History of Cape Ann: Goncalves, Joseph L." *Sawyer Free Library.* Gloucester, MA. 1978.

Goulart, Tone P. *The Holy Ghost Festas: A Historic Perspective of the Portuguese in California.* Portuguese Chamber of Commerce of California. San Jose, CA. 2002.

Greenlaw, Linda. *All Fishermen are Liars.* Hyperion. New York, NY. 2005.

————. *The Hungry Ocean: A Swordboat Captain's Journey.* Hyperion. New York, NY. 1999.

————. *The Lobster Chronicles: Life on a Very Small Island.* Hyperion. New York, NY. 2002.

————. *Sea-Worthy – A Swordboat Captain Returns to the Sea.* Penguin Books. New York, NY. 2010.

Grey, Zane. *The Gladiator of the Sea.* Start Publishing LLC. eBook

Edition. 2014.

——. *The Royal Purple Game of the Sea.* Start Publishing LLC. eBook Edition. 2014.

——. *Seven Marlin Swordfish in One Day.* Start Publishing LLC. eBook Edition. 2014.

——. *Swordfish.* Start Publishing LLC. eBook Edition. 2014.

——. *Tales of Fishes.* The Derrydale Press. Lanham, MD. 2001.

——. *Tales of Swordfish and Tuna.* The Derrydale Press. Lanham, MD. 1991.

——. *Two Fights with Swordfish.* Start Publishing LLC. eBook Edition. 2014.

Gudger, E. W. "The Perils and Romance of Swordfishing." *The Scientific Monthly.* vol 51, no 1, July 1940.

Hawes, Charles Boardman. *Gloucester by Land and Sea – The Story of a New England Seacoast Town.* Little, Brown and Company. Boston, MA. 1923.

Hemmingway, Ernest. *Hemmingway on Fishing.* The Lyons Press. New York, NY. 2000.

——. *The Old Man and the Sea.* Scribner. New York, NY. 1952.

Hicky, Walter V. *The Final Voyage of the Portland.* National Archives. Winter 2006.

"Honors Lost Fishermen." *The New York Times.* Monday, August, 24, 1925.

"Hurricane Hits Big Ocean Liners Terrific Blows." *Freeport Journal Standard*. Freeport, IL. August 28, 1924.

Junger, Sebastian. *The Perfect Storm*. W. W. Norton & Company, Inc. New York, NY. 1997.

*The King James Bible*. Project Gutenberg eBook. 2021.

Kipling, Rudyard. *Captains Courageous*. North Books. Wickford, RI. 2001.

Krueger, Alice, Interviewee, Krueger, Rose Interviewee, and Masters, David, Interviewer. "Toward an Oral History of Cape Ann: Krueger, Alice Rose." *Sawyer Free Library*. Gloucester, MA. 1978.

Kurlansky, Mark. *The Last Fish Tale: The Fate of the Atlantic and Survival in Gloucester, America's Oldest Fishing Port and Most Original Town*. Ballantine Books. New York, NY. 2008.

"Last of the Whalers Wrecked in Storm." *The New York Times*. August 27, 1924.

Leal, João. *Traveling Rituals: Azorean Holy Ghost Festivals in Southeastern New England*. Centro de Estudos de Antropologia Social. 2005.

Levesque, Juan C. "Gladiator: Swordfish Life Cycle." *Florida Sportsman*. August 27, 2014.

Lineaweaver, Thomas H. "Xiphias the Swordfish." *Sports Illustrated*. July 28, 1958.

Lodi, Edward. *Nantucket Sleigh Ride*. Rock Village Publishing. Middleborough, MA. 2005.

Longfellow, Henry Wadsworth. *The Complete Poetical Works of Henry Wadsworth Longfellow*. Buccaneer Books. Cutchogue, NY. 1993.

———. *Poems of Places*. Houghton, Osgood & Co. Boston, MA. 1837.

"Lost Life when Dory Upset on Brown's Bank." *Gloucester Daily Times and Cape Ann Advertiser*. April 13, 1925.

"Lost Man off Here Saturday." *Gloucester Daily Times and Cape Ann Advertiser*. December 22, 1924.

Madeira, José and da Silveira, António Brum. "Active tectonics and first paleoseismological results in Faial, Pico and S. Jorge islands (Azores, Portugal)." *Annals of Geophysics*. Volume. 46, Number 5. October 2003.

Maloney, Elbert S. *Chapman Piloting & Seamanship*. Hearst Books. New York, NY. 2003.

Marden, Luis. "Gloucester Blesses its Portuguese Fleet." *National Geographic Magazine*. Vol 104, No 1, July, 1953.

McEwan, Larry, Interviewee and Brayton, Linda, Interviewer. "Toward an Oral History of Cape Ann: McEwan, Larry." *Sawyer Free Library*. Gloucester, MA. 1978.

McFarland, Raymond. *The Masts of Gloucester – Recollections of a Fisherman*. W. W. Norton & Company Inc. New York, NY. 1937.

McLaren, Keith. *A Race for Real Sailors*. David R. Godine Publisher. Boston, MA. 2006.

*Memorial of the Celebration of the Two Hundred and Fiftieth Anniversary of the Incorporation of the Town of Gloucester, Mass.* Alfred Mudge & Son. August 1901.

"Memorial to Anniversary Nearly Ready." *Gloucester Daily Times and Cape Ann Advertiser.* August 12, 1925.

Morais, Christina. "Portuguese Crowning Festivities a Time of Faith and Fun." *Gloucester Times.* May 26, 2007.

Morris, John N. *Alone at Sea – Gloucester in the Age of the Dorymen (1623-1939).* Commonwealth Editions. Beverly, MA. 2010.

Munroe, Kirk. *Dorymates: A Tale of the Fishing Banks.* Harper & Brothers, Franklin Square. New York, NY. 1889.

Newell, Marilou. *The Wanderer: A Short History of the Last Whaling Bark.* Mattapoisett Historical Society. September 23, 2018.

"New Sch. Columbia Ready for Fishing." *Gloucester Daily Times and Cape Ann Advertiser.* April 25, 1923.

"Observed her 95th Birthday." *Gloucester Daily Times and Cape Ann Advertiser.* August 23, 1924.

"Old Whaler Lost." *Boston Daily Globe.* August 27, 1924.

"One Lone Trip in Port Today." *Gloucester Daily Times and Cape Ann Advertiser.* August 21, 1924.

"Parker's Deck Swept by Gale." *Gloucester Daily Times and Cape Ann Advertiser.* September 2, 1924.

"Passengers on Steamer New England Sighted Great Lizard." *Gloucester Daily Times and Cape Ann Advertiser.* July 28, 1899.

"Plan to Revive Fishermen's Race." *The New York Times.* August 25, 1924.

Pimental, Cecile N. *The Mary P. Mesquita Rundown at Sea.* The Anundsen Publishing Co. Decorah, IA. 1998.

"Plans for Defense Day Progressing." *Gloucester Daily Times and Cape Ann Advertiser.* August 27, 1924.

Pollack, Susan. *Gloucester Fishermen's Wives Cookbook.* Twin Lights Publishers, Inc. Rockport, MA. 2005.

Pringle, James R. *History of the Town and City of Gloucester, Cape Ann, Massachusetts.* Gloucester, MA. 1892.

"Rescued Due in New York Today." *Gloucester Daily Times and Cape Ann Advertiser.* June 30, 1925.

Reynolds, Josh. *The Port of Gloucester.* Commonwealth Editions. Beverly, MA. 2000.

Rogers, Francis M. *Atlantic Islanders of the Azores and Madeiras.* The Christopher Publishing House. North Quincy, MA. 1979.

*The Sailors' Magazine and Seaman's Friend.* American Seaman's Friend Society. New York, NY. OL. LXXXVII. No 1. January 1915.

——. American Seaman's Friend Society. New York, NY. OL. LXXXVII. No 2. February 1915.

——. American Seaman's Friend Society. New York, NY. OL. LXXXVII. No 3. March 1915.

——. American Seaman's Friend Society. New York, NY. OL.

LXXXVII. No 4. April 1915.

——. American Seaman's Friend Society. New York, NY. OL. LXXXVII. No 5. May 1915.

——. American Seaman's Friend Society. New York, NY. OL. LXXXVII. No 6. June 1915.

——. American Seaman's Friend Society. New York, NY. OL. LXXXVII. No 7. July 1915.

——. American Seaman's Friend Society. New York, NY. OL. LXXXVII. No 8. August 1915.

——. American Seaman's Friend Society. New York, NY. OL. LXXXVII. No 9. September 1915.

——. American Seaman's Friend Society. New York, NY. OL. LXXXVII. No 10. October 1915.

——. American Seaman's Friend Society. New York, NY. OL. LXXXVII. No 11. November 1915.

——. American Seaman's Friend Society. New York, NY. OL. LXXXVII. No 12. December 1915.

Santos, Michael Wayne. *Caught in Irons – North Atlantic Fishermen in the Last Days of Sail*. Associated University Presses. Cranbury, NJ. 2002.

"The Senior Flicker." Senior Annual. *Gloucester High*. Gloucester, MA. 1924.

——. Senior Annual. *Gloucester High*. Gloucester, MA. 1929.

Shakespeare, William. "Venus and Adonis." *Shakespeare's Masterpieces*.

Books, Inc. Publishers. New York, NY. 1940.

Sheedy, Roberta. *Out of Gloucester*. Down to the Sea in Ships. https://www.downtosea.com/

"Skipper and One of Crew Lost when Republic Sank." *Gloucester Daily Times and Cape Ann Advertiser*. February 17, 1925.

"Skipper Swept to Death in Tuesday's Big Gale." *Gloucester Daily Times and Cape Ann Advertiser*. August 29, 1924.

Soini, Wayne. *Gloucester's Sea Serpent*. The History Press. Charleston, SC. 2010.

"Soldiers and Citizens Join in Defense Day Celebration." *Gloucester Daily Times and Cape Ann Advertiser*. September 13, 1924.

"The Spring Kings – Capt. Joseph P. Mesquita and the Portuguese Crowning Ceremony." *The Herald News*. Fall River, MA. June 4, 2020.

"Stories in Time: Gloucester's Portuguese Crowning Ceremony." *Cape Ann Beacon*. Cape Ann Museum Curatorial Department. June 4, 2020.

"Storm Takes Toll of Two More Lives." *Gloucester Daily Times and Cape Ann Advertiser*. January 28, 1925.

"Storm Leaves Wreckage in its Pathway." *Biddeford Daily Journal*. Biddeford, ME. September 4, 1924.

"The Story Behind the Man at the Wheel." *Discover Gloucester*. June 30, 2018.

"Swordfish Had Attacked Craft." *Gloucester Daily Times and Cape Ann*

*Advertiser.* August 23, 1909.

"Swordfishing off Martha's Vineyard." *Forest and Stream.* New York. Volume LXXIX. July 13, 1912.

"Swordfishing Hunting in the Straits of Messina – an Ancient and Noble Battle has Become Very One Sided." *Off the Beaten Track in Palermo.* June 29, 2013.

Thomas, Gordan W. *Fast and Able: Life Stories of Great Gloucester Fishing Vessels.* Commonwealth Editions. Beverly, MA. 2002.

"Throngs Packed New Parkway During Exercises." *Gloucester Daily Times and Cape Ann Advertiser.* August 24, 1925.

"Tuesday's Hurricane Took Toll of Three More Lives." *Gloucester Daily Times and Cape Ann Advertiser.* August 30, 1924.

Twain, Mark. *The Innocents Abroad.* Signet Classics. New York, NY. 2007.

Venables, Bernard. *Baleia! Baleia! Whale Hunters of the Azores.* Alfred A. Knopf, Inc. New York, NY. 1968.

Vigor, John. *The Practical Mariner's Book of Knowledge.* International Marine/Ragged Mountain Press. Camden, ME. 1994.

"The Wanderer Sails on Last Voyage." *The New York Times.* August 26, 1924.

"Will Be Given Tryout Today." *Gloucester Daily Times and Cape Ann Advertiser.* August 23, 1924.

Wright, John Hardy. *Gloucester and Rockport - Images of America.* Arcadia

Publishing. Charleston, SC. 2000.

"Yesterday's Storm and Gale Did Much Damage on Cape." *Gloucester Daily Times and Cape Ann Advertiser.* August 27, 1924.